SQL Short Course

CHRIS FEHILY

Questing Vole Press

SQL Short Course
by Chris Fehily

Editor: Kevin Debenjak
Proofreader: Pat Kissell
Compositor: Hiromi Yamada
Cover: Questing Vole Press

Contents

CHAPTER 1

Introduction

This book is for analysts, developers, data scientists, Microsoft Office users, and anyone else who wants a good working knowledge of SQL, the most widely used programming language for interacting with databases.

Each chapter contains a single learn-by-example lesson. The SQL programming lessons start with simple data retrieval and sorting, move on to filtering and grouping, and then build to more-advanced topics, including joins, subqueries, views, and transactions.

SQL, Briefly

SQL (pronounced *es-kyoo-el*) is the standard programming language for creating, updating, and retrieving information that's stored in databases. With SQL, you can turn your ordinary questions ("Where do our customers live?") into statements that your database system can understand (`SELECT DISTINCT city, state FROM customers;`). You can also use SQL to add, change, and delete data and database objects. All modern relational database management systems (DBMSs) support SQL, although support varies by product (more about this in the next section).

SQL, like any programming language, is defined by rules of **syntax**, which determine the words and symbols you can use and how they can be combined, and **semantics**, which determine the actual meaning of a syntactically correct statement. Note that you can write a legal SQL statement that expresses the wrong meaning (good syntax, bad semantics). Chapter 3 introduces SQL syntax and semantics.

SQL statements read like sentences and are fairly easy to understand, particularly when compared with other programming languages. A novice programmer probably would understand the SQL statement `SELECT au_fname, au_lname FROM authors ORDER BY au_lname;` to mean "List the authors' first and last names, sorted by last name," whereas the same person would find the equivalent C or Perl program impenetrable.

SQL isn't "owned" by any particular firm. It's an open standard defined by an international standards working group, under the joint leadership of the International Organization for Standardization (ISO) and the International Engineering Consortium (IEC). The American National Standards Institute (ANSI) participates in the working groups and has ratified the standard.

Tip: It's a common misconception that SQL stands for *structured query language*; it stands for S–Q–L and nothing else. The official ISO/IEC name is Database Language SQL.

SQL is used to change data and database objects. The SELECT, INSERT, UPDATE, and DELETE statements, for example, retrieve, reckon, insert, edit, and delete data stored in a database. The CREATE, ALTER, and DROP statements create, modify, and destroy database objects such as tables, indexes, and views. Database administrators also use SQL to authorize certain users to view, change, or delete data and database objects. The GRANT statement assigns privileges to users and roles (a **role** is a named set of privileges). The REVOKE statement removes privileges.

DBMSs Covered in This Book

This book covers the following DBMSs:

- Microsoft Access
- Microsoft SQL Server
- Oracle
- IBM DB2
- MySQL
- PostgreSQL

To run SQL programs in one of these DBMSs, see Appendix B (page 217). If you're using a different DBMS and one of the SQL examples doesn't work, read the documentation to see how your DBMS's SQL implementation departs from the SQL standard.

Using SQL with a specific DBMS

DBMS The DBMS icon flags a vendor-specific departure from the SQL standard. If you see this icon, it means that a particular vendor's SQL dialect doesn't comply with the standard, and you must modify the listed SQL program to run on your DBMS. For example, the standard SQL operator that joins (concatenates) two strings is || (a double pipe), but Microsoft products use + (a plus sign) and MySQL uses the CONCAT() function instead, so you'll need to change all occurrences of a||b in the example SQL listing to a + b (if you're using Microsoft Access or Microsoft SQL Server) or to CONCAT(a,b) (if you're using MySQL). In most cases, the SQL examples will work as is or with minor syntactic changes. Occasionally, SQL code won't work at all because the DBMS doesn't support a particular feature.

Database vs. DBMS

A database is not the same as the database software that you're running; it's incorrect to say, "Oracle is a database." Database software is called a **database management system (DBMS)**. A **database**, which is just one component of a DBMS, is the data itself—that is, it's a container (one or more files) that stores structured information. Besides controlling the organization, integrity, and retrieval of data in databases, DBMSs handle tasks such as physical storage, security, backup, replication, and error recovery. DBMS also is abbreviated **RDBMS**, in which the *R* stands for *relational*.

Conventions Used in This Book

I use the following typographic conventions:

Bold type introduces new terms.

Italic type represents replaceable variables in regular text.

`Monospace type` denotes SQL code and syntax in listings and in regular text. It also shows command-prompt text.

`Bold monospace type` highlights SQL code fragments and results that are explained in the accompanying text.

`Italic monospace type` denotes a variable in SQL code that you must replace with a value. You'd replace *`column`* with the name of an actual column, for example.

Syntax conventions

SQL is a free-form language without restrictions on line breaks or the number of words per line, so I use a consistent style in SQL syntax diagrams and code listings to make the code easy to read and maintain:

- Each SQL statement begins on a new line.
- The indentation level is two spaces.
- Each clause of a statement begins on a new, indented line:

  ```
  SELECT au_fname, au_lname
    FROM authors
    ORDER BY au_lname;
  ```

- SQL is case insensitive, meaning that *myname*, *MyName*, and *MYNAME* are considered to be identical identifiers. I use UPPERCASE for SQL keywords such as SELECT, NULL, and CHARACTER (see "SQL Syntax" on page 16), and lowercase or lower_case for user-defined values, such as table, column, and alias names.

  (User-defined identifiers are case sensitive when quoted and in a few other situations for some DBMSs, so it's safest to respect identifier case in SQL programs.)

- All quote marks in SQL code are straight quotes (such as ' and "), not curly, or smart, quotes (such as ’ and “). Curly quotes prevent code from working.
- Table 1.1 shows special symbols that I use in syntax diagrams.

Table 1.1 Syntax Symbols

<table>
<tr><th>Characters</th><th>Description</th></tr>
<tr><td>|</td><td>The vertical-bar or pipe symbol separates alternative items. You can choose exactly one of the given items. (Don't type the vertical bar.) A|B|C is read "A or B or C". Don't confuse the pipe symbol with the double-pipe symbol, ||, which is SQL's string-concatenation operator.</td></tr>
<tr><td>[ ]</td><td>Brackets enclose one or more optional items. (Don't type the brackets.) [A|B|C] means "type A or B or C or type nothing". [D] means "type D or type nothing".</td></tr>
<tr><td>{ }</td><td>Braces enclose one or more required items. (Don't type the braces.) {A|B|C} means "type A or B or C".</td></tr>
<tr><td>...</td><td>Ellipses mean that the preceding item(s) can be repeated any number of times.</td></tr>
</table>

Server vs. Desktop DBMSs

A **server** DBMS acts as the server part of a client/server network; it stores databases and responds to SQL requests made by many clients. A **client** is an application or computer that sends an SQL request to a server and accepts the server's response. The server does the actual work of executing the SQL against a database; the client merely accepts the answer. If your network uses a client/server architecture, the client is the computer on your desk, and the server is a powerful, specialized machine in another room, building, or country. The rules that describe how client/server requests and responses are transmitted are part of DBMS protocols and interfaces such as ODBC, JDBC, and ADO.NET.

A **desktop** DBMS is a stand-alone program that can store a database and do all the SQL processing itself or behave as a client of a server. A desktop DBMS can't accept requests from other clients (that is, it can't act like a server).

Servers include Microsoft SQL Server, Oracle, DB2, MySQL, and PostgreSQL. Desktop systems include Microsoft Access and FileMaker Pro. By convention, I use *client* and *server* to refer to client and server software itself or to the machine on which the software runs, unless the distinction is important.

CHAPTER 2

Database Basics

To be a good SQL programmer, you must be familiar with the standard data model for organizing and managing data, called the **relational model**. The foundation of this model, **set theory**, makes you think in terms of sets of data rather than individual items or rows of data. The model describes how to perform common algebraic operations (such as unions and intersections) on database tables in much the same way that they're performed on mathematical sets.

The Venn diagram below expresses the results of operations on sets. The rectangle (U) represents the universe, and the circles (A and B) inside represent sets of objects. The relative position and overlap of the circles indicate relationships between sets. In the relational model, the circles are tables, and the rectangle is all the information in a database.

Tables are analogues of sets: they're collections of distinct elements having common properties. A mathematical set would contain positive integers, for example, whereas a database table would contain information about books.

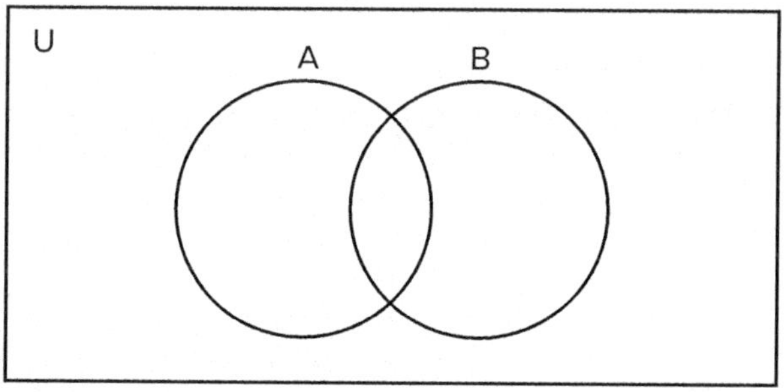

If you're familiar with databases already, you've heard alternative terms for similar concepts. Table 2.1 shows how these terms are related. Relational-model terms are in the first column; standard SQL terms are in the second column; and the third-column terms are holdovers from traditional (non-relational) file processing. I use SQL terms in this book.

Table 2.1 Similar Concepts

Model	SQL	Files
Relation	Table	File
Attribute	Column	Field
Tuple	Row	Record

Tables

From a user's point of view, a database is a collection of one or more tables (and nothing but tables). A **table**:

- Is the database structure that holds data.
- Contains data about a specific **entity type**. An entity type is a class of distinguishable real-world objects, events, or concepts with common properties—patients, movies, genes, weather conditions, invoices, projects, or appointments, for example. (Patients and appointments are different entities, so you'd store information about them in different tables.)
- Is a two-dimensional grid characterized by **rows** and **columns**.
- Holds a data item called a **value** at each row–column intersection.
- Has at least one column and zero or more rows. A table with no rows is an **empty table**.
- Has a unique name within a database (or, strictly speaking, within a schema).

Tip: The resemblance of spreadsheets to tables is superficial. Unlike a spreadsheet, a table doesn't depend on row and column order, doesn't perform calculations, doesn't allow free-form data entry, strictly checks each value's validity, and is related easily to other tables.

The grid in the following figure is an abstract representation of a table.

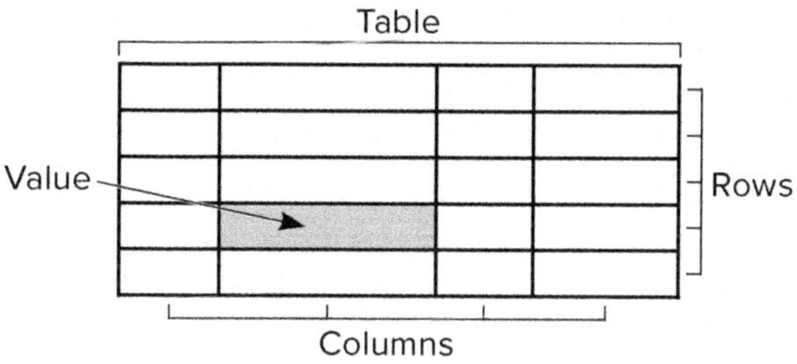

The following grid represents an actual (not abstract) table, shown as it usually appears in database software and books. This table has 3 columns, 4 rows, and 3 × 4 = 12 values. The top "row" is not a row but a header that displays column names.

```
au_id au_fname      au_lname
----- ------------- -------------
A01   Sarah         Buchman
A02   Wendy         Heydemark
A03   Hallie        Hull
A04   Klee          Hull
```

Rows and columns are said to be **unordered**, meaning that their order in a table is irrelevant for informational purposes. Interchanging columns or rows does not change the meaning of the table; the following table conveys the same information as the preceding one.

```
au_lname      au_id au_fname
------------- ----- -------------
Hull          A04   Klee
Buchman       A01   Sarah
Hull          A03   Hallie
Heydemark     A02   Wendy
```

Tip: Tables have the attractive property of **closure**, which guarantees that you'll get another table as a result no matter how you split or merge tables. This property lets you chain any number of table operations or nest them to any depth.

Columns

Columns in a given table have these characteristics:

- Each column represents a specific attribute (or property) of the table's entity type. In a table *employees*, a column named *hire_date* might show when an employee was hired, for example.
- Each column has a domain that restricts the set of values allowed in that column. A **domain** is a set of constraints that includes restrictions on a value's data type, length, format, range, uniqueness, specific values, and nullability (whether the value can be null or not). You can't insert the string value 'john' into the column *hire_date*, for example, if *hire_date* requires a valid date value. Furthermore, you can't insert just any date if *hire_date*'s range is further constrained to fall between the date that the company started and today's date. You can define a domain by using data types (Appendix C) and constraints (Chapter 21).
- Entries in columns are single-valued (atomic), meaning they're perceived to be indivisible from the point of view of database users.
- The order of columns (left to right) is unimportant.
- Each column has a name that identifies it uniquely within a table. (You can reuse the same column name in other tables.)

Rows

Rows in a given table have these characteristics:

- Each row describes a fact about an **entity**, which is a unique instance of an entity type—a particular student or appointment, for example.
- Each row contains a value or null for each of the table's columns.
- The order of rows (top to bottom) is unimportant.
- No two rows in a table can be identical.
- Each row in a table is identified uniquely by its primary key.

In practice, the number of rows in a table changes frequently, but the number of columns changes rarely. Database complexity makes adding or dropping columns difficult; column changes can affect keys, referential integrity, privileges, and so on. Inserting or deleting rows doesn't affect these things.

Primary Keys

Every value in a database must be accessible. Values are stored at row–column intersections in tables, so a value's location must refer to a specific table, column, and row. You can identify a table or column by its unique name. Rows are unnamed, however, and need a different identification mechanism called a primary key. A **primary key** is:

- *Required*. Every table has exactly one primary key. Remember that the relational model sees a table as an unordered set of rows. Because there's no concept of a "next" or "previous" row, you can't identify rows by position; without a primary key, some data would be inaccessible.
- *Unique*. Because a primary key identifies a single row in a table, no two rows in a table can have the same primary-key value.
- *Simple or composite*. A primary key has one or more columns in a table; a one-column key is called a **simple key**, and a multiple-column key is called a **composite key**.
- *Not null*. A primary-key value can't be empty. For composite keys, no column's value can be empty; see "Nulls" on page 22.
- *Stable*. Once created, a primary-key value seldom if ever changes. If an entity is deleted, its primary-key value isn't reused for a new entity.
- *Minimal*. A primary key includes only the column(s) necessary for uniqueness.

A database designer designates each table's primary key. This process is crucial because the consequence of a poor key choice is the inability to add data (rows) to a table. Suppose that you need to choose a primary key for the following table.

```
au_id au_fname      au_lname
----- ------------- -------------
A01   Sarah         Buchman
A02   Wendy         Heydemark
A03   Hallie        Hull
A04   Klee          Hull
```

The columns *au_fname* and *au_lname* separately won't work, because each one violates the uniqueness requirement. Combining *au_fname* and *au_lname* into a composite key won't work, because two authors might share a name. Names generally make poor keys because they're unstable (people divorce, companies merge, spellings change). The correct choice is *au_id*, which I invented to identify authors uniquely. Database designers create unique identifiers when natural or obvious ones (such as names) won't work.

After a primary key is defined, your DBMS will enforce the integrity of table data. You can't insert the following row, because the *au_id* value A02 already exists in the table:

```
A02    Christian    Kells
```

Nor can you insert this row, because *au_id* can't be null:

```
NULL   Christian    Kells
```

This row is legal:

```
A05    Christian    Kells
```

Tips for primary keys

- In practice, the primary key is often placed in a table's initial (leftmost) column(s). When a column name contains *id*, *key*, *code*, or *num*, it's a clue that the column might be a primary key or part of one (or a foreign key, described in the next section).
- Database designers often forgo common unique identifiers such as Social Security numbers for U.S. citizens. Instead, they use artificial keys that encode internal information that is meaningful inside the database users' organization. An employee ID, for example, might embed the year that the person was hired. Other reasons, such as privacy concerns, also spur the use of artificial keys.
- Database designers might have a choice of several unique **candidate keys** in a table, one of which is designated the primary key. After designation, the remaining candidate keys become **alternate keys**. Candidate keys often have non-nullable, unique constraints (Chapter 21).
- You *could* use *au_id* and, say, *au_lname* as a composite key, but that combination violates the minimality criterion. For an example of a composite primary key, see the table *title_authors* in Appendix A.
- DBMSs provide data types and attributes that provide unique identification values automatically for each row (such as an integer that autoincrements when a new row is inserted). See "Unique Identifiers" on page 254.

Foreign Keys

Information about different entities is stored in different tables, so you need a way to navigate between tables. The relational model provides a mechanism called a **foreign key** to associate tables. A foreign key has these characteristics:

- It's a column (or group of columns) in a table whose values relate to, or reference, values in some other table.
- It ensures that rows in one table have corresponding rows in another table.
- The table that contains the foreign key is the **referencing** or **child** table. The other table is the **referenced** or **parent** table.
- A foreign key establishes a direct relationship to the parent table's primary key (or any candidate key), so foreign-key values are restricted to existing parent-key values. This constraint is called **referential integrity**. A particular row in a table *appointments* must have an associated row in a table *patients*, for example, or there would be appointments for patients who don't exist or can't be identified. An **orphan row** is a row in a child table for which no associated parent-table row exists. In a properly designed database, you can't insert new orphan rows or make orphans out of existing child-table rows by deleting associated rows in the parent table.
- The values in the foreign key have the same domain as the parent key. Recall from "Columns" on page 10 that a domain defines the set of valid values for a column.
- Unlike primary-key values, foreign-key values can be null (empty).
- A foreign key can have a different column name than its parent key.
- Foreign-key values generally aren't unique in their own table.
- I've made a simplification in the first point: in reality, a foreign key can reference the primary key of its *own* table (rather than only some other table). A table *employees* with the primary key *emp_id* can have a foreign key *boss_id*, for example, that references the column *emp_id*. This type of table is called **self-referencing**.

The figure below shows a primary- and foreign-key relationship between two tables. The column *pub_id* is a foreign key of the table *titles* that references the column *pub_id* of *publishers*.

After a foreign key is defined, your DBMS will enforce referential integrity. You can't insert the following row into the child table *titles*, because the *pub_id* value P05 doesn't exist in the parent table *publishers*:

```
T07     I Blame My Mother     P05
```

You can insert this row only if the foreign key accepts nulls:

```
T07     I Blame My Mother     NULL
```

This row is legal:

```
T07     I Blame My Mother     P03
```

Tip: Allowing nulls (page 22) in a foreign-key column complicates enforcement of referential integrity. In practice, nulls in a foreign key often remain null temporarily, pending a real-life decision or discovery.

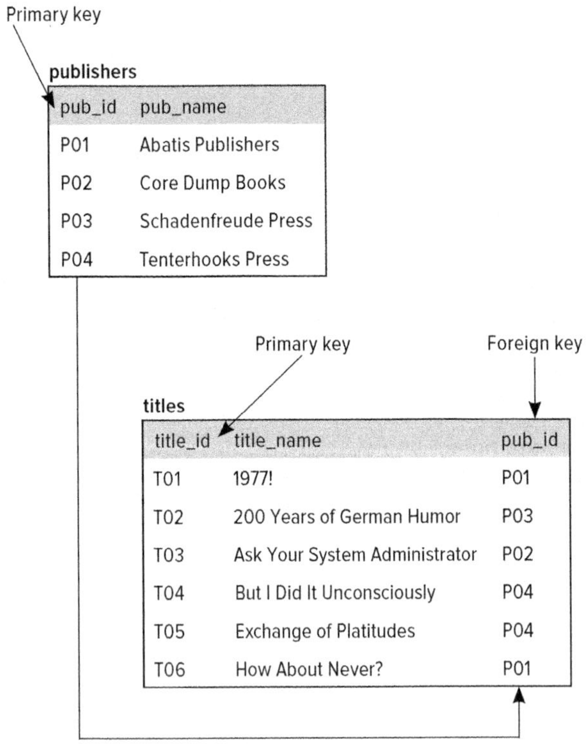

CHAPTER 3

SQL Basics

An SQL program is a sequence of SQL statements executed in order. This chapter teaches you the rules that govern SQL syntax, which you must use to write SQL programs.

SQL Syntax

The following figure shows an example SQL statement. Don't worry about the meaning (semantics) of the statement; I'm using it to explain SQL syntax.

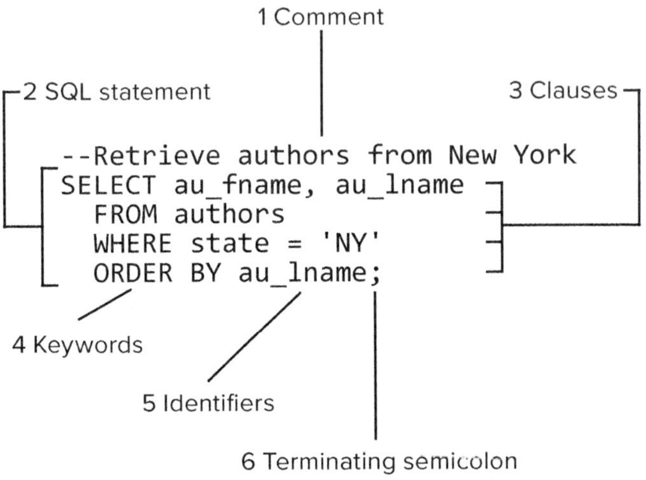

1 **Comment**. A **comment** is optional text that explains your program. Comments usually describe what a program does and how, or why code was changed. Comments are for humans—the DBMS ignores them. A comment is introduced by two consecutive hyphens and continues until the end of the line. Some DBMSs support bracketed comments, which start with /*, continue over one or more lines, and end with */.

2 **SQL statement**. An SQL statement is a valid combination of tokens introduced by a keyword. **Tokens** are the basic indivisible particles of the SQL language; they can't be reduced grammatically. Tokens include keywords, identifiers, operators, literals (constants), and punctuation symbols.

3 **Clauses**. An SQL statement has one or more clauses. In general, a **clause** is a fragment of an SQL statement that's introduced by a keyword, is required or optional, and must be given in a particular order. SELECT, FROM, WHERE, and ORDER BY introduce the four clauses in this example.

4 **Keywords**. A **keyword** is a word that SQL reserves because it has special meaning in the language. Using a keyword outside its specific context (as an identifier, for example) causes an error. DBMSs use a mix

of standard and nonstandard keywords; search your DBMS documentation for *keywords* or *reserved words*. The keywords in this example are SELECT, FROM, WHERE, ORDER, and BY.

5 **Identifiers. Identifiers** are words that you (or the database designer) use to name database objects such as tables, columns, aliases, indexes, and views. The identifiers in this example are *au_fname*, *au_lname*, *authors*, and *state*. For more information, see "Identifiers" on page 20.

6 **Terminating semicolon**. An SQL statement ends with a semicolon.

SQL is a free-form language whose statements can:

- Be in uppercase or lowercase. (SELECT, select, and sElEcT are considered to be identical keywords, for example.)
- Continue on the next line as long as you don't split words, tokens, or quoted strings in two.
- Be on the same line as other statements.
- Start in any column.

Despite this flexibility, you should adopt a consistent style. There aren't many rules about how to format an SQL statement. The following statement is equivalent to the one in the preceding figure.

```
select au_fname
  ,         AU_LNAME
              FROM
 authors WhErE     state
= 'NY' order
              bY
AU_lnamE
      ;
```

I use uppercase keywords and lowercase identifiers and indent each clause on its own line; see "Conventions Used in This Book" on page 4 for my typographic and syntax conventions.

Tip: Distinguish between a SELECT *statement*, which is the entire statement from SELECT to semicolon, and a SELECT *clause*, which is the part of the SELECT statement that lists the output columns.

Common Errors

Some common SQL programming errors are:

- Omitting the terminating semicolon
- Misspelling a keyword or identifier
- Mismatched or unmatched parentheses or quotes
- Listing clauses out of order
- Not surrounding a string or datetime literal with single quotes
- Surrounding a numeric literal or the keyword NULL with quotes
- Mismatching a table and column (typing `SELECT royalty_share FROM authors` instead of `SELECT royalty_share FROM title_authors`, for example)

These errors usually are easy to catch and correct, even if your DBMS returns an obscure or unhelpful error message. Remember that the real error actually can occur well before the statement the DBMS flags as an error. For example, if you run

```
CREATE TABLE misspelled_name
```

your DBMS will go right ahead and create a table with the bad name. Your error won't show up until later, when you try to reference the table with, say,

```
SELECT * FROM correct_name
```

Tip: A common way to test and fix (debug) SQL programs is to use comments to temporarily stop SQL code from being executed. If you're working on a long SQL statement and want to test only part of it, you can **comment out** some of the code so that the DBMS sees it as comments and ignores it.

Expressions

An **expression** is any legal combination of symbols that evaluates to a single data value. You can combine mathematical or logical operators, identifiers, literals, functions, column names, aliases, and so on. Table 3.1 lists some common expressions and examples. These expressions are covered in more detail later.

Table 3.1 Types of Expressions

<table>
<tr><th>Type</th><th>Example</th></tr>
<tr><td>Case</td><td><code>CASE WHEN n <> 0 THEN x/n ELSE 0 END</code></td></tr>
<tr><td>Cast</td><td><code>CAST(pubdate AS CHARACTER)</code></td></tr>
<tr><td>Datetime value</td><td><code>start_time + '01:30'</code></td></tr>
<tr><td>Numeric value</td><td><code>(sales*price)/12</code></td></tr>
<tr><td>String value</td><td><code>'Dear '||au_fname||','</code></td></tr>
</table>

Identifiers

An **identifier** is a name that lets you refer to an object unambiguously within the hierarchy of database objects (whether a schema, database, column, key, index, view, constraint, or anything created with a CREATE statement). An identifier must be unique within its **scope**, which defines where and when it can be referenced. In general:

- Database names must be unique on a specified instance of a database server.
- Table and view names must be unique within a given database (or schema).
- Column, key, index, and constraint names must be unique within a given table or view.

These rules let you duplicate names for objects whose scopes don't overlap. You can give the same name to columns in different tables, for example, or to tables in different databases.

DBMS DBMS scopes vary in the extent to which they require identifier names to be unique. **SQL Server**, for example, requires an index name to be unique for only its table, whereas **Oracle** and **DB2** require an index name to be unique throughout the database. Search your DBMS documentation for *identifiers* or *names*.

Standard SQL has the following **identifier rules** for names:

- Can be up to 128 characters long
- Must begin with a letter
- Can contain letters, digits, and underscores (_)
- Can't contain spaces or special characters (such as #, $, &, %, or punctuation)
- Can't be reserved keywords (except for quoted identifiers)

Standard SQL distinguishes between reserved and non-reserved keywords. You can't use **reserved keywords** as identifiers because they have special meaning in SQL. You can't name a table "select" or a column "sum", for example. **Non-reserved keywords** have a special meaning in only some contexts and can be used as identifiers in other contexts. Most non-reserved keywords actually are the names of built-in tables and functions, so it's safest never to use them as identifiers either.

You can use a **quoted identifier**, also called a **delimited identifier**, to break some of SQL's identifier rules. A quoted identifier is a name surrounded by double quotes. The name can contain spaces and special characters, is case sensitive, and can be a reserved keyword. Quoted identifiers can annoy other programmers and cause problems with third-party and even a vendor's own tools, so using them usually is a bad idea.

Here's some more advice for choosing identifier names:

- Stick to the standard rules even if your DBMS has less restrictive ones (**Oracle** names can contain # and $ symbols, for example).
- In some cases, your DBMS will be more restrictive than the standard (**MySQL** identifiers can be up to only 64 characters long, for example).
- Use lowercase letters.
- *names_with_underscores* are easier to read than *nameswithoutthem*.
- Use consistent names and abbreviations throughout the database—pick either emp or employee and stick with it.

Although you can't use (unquoted) reserved words as identifiers, you *can* embed them in identifiers. *group* and *max* are illegal identifiers, for example, but *groups* and *max_price* are valid. If you're worried that your identifier might be a reserved word in some other SQL dialect, just add an underscore to the end of the name (*element_*, for example); no reserved keyword ends with an underscore.

DBMS You can surround **SQL Server** quoted identifiers with double quotes or brackets ([]); brackets are preferred. In **DB2**, you can use reserved words as identifiers (but doing so isn't a good idea because your program won't be portable). **MySQL** ANSI_QUOTES mode allows double-quoted identifiers. DBMSs have their own nonstandard keywords; search your DBMS documentation for *keywords* or *reserved words*.

In **MySQL**, the case sensitivity of the underlying operating system determines the case sensitivity of database and table names.

The SQL standard directs DBMSs to convert identifier names to uppercase internally. So in the guts of your SQL compiler, the unquoted identifier *myname* is equivalent to the quoted identifier *"MYNAME"* (not *"myname"*). **PostgreSQL** doesn't conform to the standard and converts to *lowercase*. To write portable programs, always quote a particular name or never quote it (don't mix styles). DBMSs aren't consistent when it comes to case sensitivity, so the best practice is always to respect case for user-defined identifiers.

Nulls

When your data are incomplete, you can use a null to represent a missing or unknown value. A **null** has these characteristics (which are covered in more detail when they arise):

- In SQL statements, the keyword NULL represents a null.
- A null is used for a value that might never be known, might be determined later, or is inapplicable. (Think of a null as a marker or flag for a missing value, rather than as a value itself.)
- A null differs from zero, a string that contains only spaces, or an empty string (''). A null in the column *price* doesn't mean that an item has no price or that its price is zero; it means that the price is unknown or has not been set. (**Oracle** is a special case with respect to empty strings; see the DBMS Tip in this section.)
- Nulls can appear in columns of any data type that are not restricted by NOT NULL or PRIMARY KEY constraints (Chapter 21). Nulls should not be allowed in alternate keys.
- **Nullable** means that a column is allowed to contain nulls. The CREATE TABLE and ALTER TABLE statements set a column's nullability.
- To detect nulls, see "Testing for Nulls with IS NULL" on page 61.
- Nulls aren't equal (or unequal) to each other. You can't determine whether a null matches any other value, including another null, so the expressions NULL = *any_value*, NULL <> *any_value*, NULL = NULL, and NULL <> NULL are neither true nor false but unknown.
- Although nulls are never equal to each other, DISTINCT (page 29) treats all the nulls in a particular column as duplicates.
- When you sort a column that contains nulls, the nulls will be either greater than or less than all the non-null values, depending on the DBMS. See "Sorting and Nulls" on page 35.
- Nulls propagate through computations. The result of any arithmetic expression or operation that involves a null is null: (12*NULL)/4 is null.
- Most aggregate functions (Chapter 13), such as SUM(), AVG(), and MAX(), ignore nulls. COUNT(*) is an exception.
- If the grouping column in a GROUP BY clause (Chapter 14) contains nulls, all the nulls are put in a single group.
- Nulls affect the results of joins, and can cause problems in subqueries.

Tips for nulls

- Use caution when interpreting results in which nulls are involved. Nulls cause so many problems and complications—I've listed some important ones here—that some database experts urge users to minimize their use or not use them at all (and instead use default values or some other missing-data scheme). Nevertheless, you won't become a competent SQL programmer without understanding nulls.
- The term *null value* is inaccurate—a null indicates the *lack* of a value.
- Don't place the keyword NULL in quotes; your DBMS will interpret it as the character string 'NULL' rather than as a null.
- If nulls appear in a column because actual values are not meaningful (rather than unknown), you can split the column off into its own table with a one-to-one relationship with the other table. In the following figure, the original table *employees* has the column *commission*, which specifies an employee's sales commission. *commission* contains mostly nulls because most employees aren't salespeople. To avoid the proliferation of nulls, I've moved *commission* to its own table.

employees

emp_id	emp_name	commission
E01	Eli McLemore	NULL
E02	Monty Wendt	0.25
E03	Damien Shaw	NULL
E04	Russell Sager	NULL
E05	Jill Stallworth	NULL
E06	Pamela Gant	0.08

employees

emp_id	emp_name
E01	Eli McLemore
E02	Monty Wendt
E03	Damien Shaw
E04	Russell Sager
E05	Jill Stallworth
E06	Pamela Gant

commissions

emp_id	commission
E02	0.25
E06	0.08

- You can get a null from a column that doesn't allow nulls. The column *au_id* in the table *authors* doesn't allow nulls, but the following SELECT statement returns a null for the maximum *au_id*.

  ```
  SELECT MAX(au_id)
    FROM authors
    WHERE au_lname = 'XXX';
  ```

  The result is:

  ```
  MAX(au_id)
  ----------
  NULL
  ```

- **DBMS** The display of nulls in results varies by DBMS. A null might appear as NULL, (NULL), <NULL>, -, or empty space, for example.

  Oracle treats an empty string ('') as a null. This treatment might not continue to be true in future releases, however, and Oracle recommends that you do not treat empty strings the same as nulls in your SQL code. This behavior can cause conversion problems among DBMSs. In the sample database, for example, the column *au_fname* in the table *authors* is defined as NOT NULL. In Oracle, the first name of the author Kellsey (author A06) is a space (' '); in the other DBMSs, the first name is an empty string ('').

CHAPTER 4

Retrieving Data from a Table

The SELECT Statement

SQL's workhorse is the SELECT statement. Most SQL work involves retrieving and manipulating data by using this one (albeit complex) statement. SELECT retrieves rows, columns, and derived values from one or more tables in a database; its syntax is:

```
SELECT columns
  FROM tables
  [JOIN joins]
  [WHERE search_condition]
  [GROUP BY grouping_columns]
  [HAVING search_condition]
  [ORDER BY sort_columns];
```

The SELECT and FROM clauses are covered in this chapter, and the other clauses—WHERE, ORDER BY, GROUP BY, and so on—are covered in later chapters.

By convention, I call only a SELECT statement a *query* because it returns a result set. DBMS documentation and other books might refer to *any* SQL statement as a query. Although SELECT is powerful, it's not dangerous: you can't use it to add, change, or delete data or database objects.

Tip: Recall that *italic_type* denotes a variable in code that must be replaced with a value, and brackets indicate an optional clause or item; see "Conventions Used in This Book" on page 4 for typographic and syntax conventions.

Retrieving Columns with SELECT and FROM

In its simplest form, a SELECT statement retrieves columns from a table; you can retrieve one column, multiple columns, or all columns. The SELECT clause lists the columns to display, and the FROM clause specifies the table from which to draw the columns.

To retrieve a single column from a table, specify the column name and the name of the table that contains the column. To list the cities in which the authors live, for example, type:

```
SELECT city
  FROM authors;
```

The result is:

```
city
-------------
Bronx
Boulder
San Francisco
San Francisco
New York
Palo Alto
Sarasota
```

To retrieve multiple columns from a table, specify two or more comma-separated column names in the SELECT clause:

```
SELECT au_fname, au_lname, city, state
  FROM authors;
```

The result is:

```
au_fname  au_lname    city          state
--------- ----------- ------------- -----
Sarah     Buchman     Bronx         NY
Wendy     Heydemark   Boulder       CO
Hallie    Hull        San Francisco CA
Klee      Hull        San Francisco CA
Christian Kells       New York      NY
          Kellsey     Palo Alto     CA
Paddy     O'Furniture Sarasota      FL
```

Note that columns are displayed in the same order in which they're listed in the SELECT clause, not the order in which they're defined in the table.

To retrieve all columns from a table, use the asterisk (*) wildcard character instead of actual column names:

```
SELECT *
  FROM authors;
```

When a wildcard (*) is specified, columns are displayed in the order in which they're defined in the table. SELECT * is often risky because the number or order of a table's columns can change and cause your program to fail. Likewise, SELECT * won't be understood by people unfamiliar with the table's columns. In contrast to queries that name specific columns in the SELECT clause, SELECT * is a resource hog that drags unneeded data across networks.

Results are Unformatted

All results display raw, unformatted values. Monetary amounts lack currency signs, and numbers might have too many decimal places, for example. Reporting tools—not data-retrieval tools—format data, although DBMSs have nonstandard functions that let you format text, numbers, and datetimes in query results. See **Microsoft SQL Server**'s datename() function or **MySQL**'s date_format() function, for example.

Following Along with the Examples

The example SQL statements in this book use the database described in Appendix A, "The Sample Database". If you'd like to follow along and try the examples yourself, refer to Appendix A for instructions on how to download and create this database. To run SQL programs on the DBMSs covered in this book, refer to Appendix B, "Running SQL Programs".

Creating Column Aliases with AS

In the preceding query results, I let the DBMS use default values for column headings. (A column's default heading in a result is the source column's name in the table definition.) You can use the AS clause to create a column alias. A **column alias** is an alternative name (identifier) that you specify to control how column headings are displayed in a result. Use column aliases if column names are cryptic, hard to type, too long, or too short.

A column alias immediately follows a column name in the SELECT clause of a SELECT statement. Enclose the alias in single or double quotes if it's a reserved keyword or if it contains spaces, punctuation, or special characters. You can omit the quotes if the alias is a single non-reserved word that contains only letters, digits, or underscores. If you want a particular column to retain its default heading, omit its AS clause.

The following statement shows the syntactic variations of the AS clause:

```
SELECT
    au_fname AS "First name",
    au_lname AS 'Last name',
    city AS City,
    state,
    zip 'Postal code'
  FROM authors;
```

The result is:

```
First name Last name   City          state Postal code
---------- ----------- ------------- ----- -----------
Sarah      Buchman     Bronx         NY    10468
Wendy      Heydemark   Boulder       CO    80303
Hallie     Hull        San Francisco CA    94123
Klee       Hull        San Francisco CA    94123
Christian  Kells       New York      NY    10014
           Kellsey     Palo Alto     CA    94305
Paddy      O'Furniture Sarasota      FL    34236
```

In standard SQL and most DBMSs, the keyword AS is optional, but you should include it and surround aliases with double quotes to make your SQL code more portable and readable.

You can use a reserved keyword if you quote the alias. The query `SELECT SUM(sales) AS "Sum" FROM titles;` uses the reserved word SUM as a column alias, for example. For information about keywords, see "SQL Syntax" on page 16 and "Identifiers" on page 20.

DBMS **Microsoft Access** and **PostgreSQL** require the AS keyword for column references.

Oracle and **DB2** display unquoted column names and aliases in uppercase.

sqlplus (**Oracle**'s command-line processor) truncates column aliases to the number of characters specified in the table's column definitions. The column alias *"Postal code"* displays as *Posta* in a CHAR(5) column, for example.

DBMSs have restrictions on embedded spaces, punctuation, and special characters in aliases; search your DBMS documentation for *SELECT* or *AS*.

Eliminating Duplicate Rows with DISTINCT

Columns often contain duplicate values, and it's common to want a result that lists each duplicate only once. The result of the statement:

```
SELECT state
  FROM authors;
```

contains unneeded duplicates of CA and NY:

```
state
-----
NY
CO
CA
CA
NY
CA
FL
```

The DISTINCT keyword eliminates duplicate rows from a result. To list the distinct states in which the authors live, type:

```
SELECT DISTINCT state
  FROM authors;
```

The result is:

```
state
-----
NY
CO
CA
FL
```

If the SELECT DISTINCT clause contains more than one column, the values of *all* the specified columns combined determine the uniqueness of rows. For example, the statement:

```
SELECT DISTINCT city, state
  FROM authors;
```

eliminates two-column duplicates (it's the city–state combination that's considered to be unique, not the value in any single column).

The result is:

```
city          state
------------- -----
Bronx         NY
Boulder       CO
New York      NY
Palo Alto     CA
San Francisco CA
Sarasota      FL
```

Note that if a table has a properly defined primary key, `SELECT DISTINCT * FROM table;` and `SELECT * FROM table;` return identical results because all rows are unique.

Tip: For DISTINCT operations, the DBMS performs an internal sort to identify and remove duplicate rows. Sorting is computationally expensive—don't use DISTINCT if you don't have to.

DISTINCT and Nulls

Although nulls (page 22) never equal each other because their values are unknown, DISTINCT considers all nulls to be duplicates of each other. SELECT DISTINCT returns only one null in a result, regardless of how many nulls it encounters.

CHAPTER 5

Sorting Rows

The ORDER BY Clause

Rows in a query result are unordered, so you should view the order in which rows appear as being arbitrary. This situation arises because the relational model posits that row order is irrelevant for table operations. You can use the ORDER BY clause to sort rows by a specified column or columns in ascending (lowest to highest) or descending (highest to lowest) order. The ORDER BY clause is always the last clause in a SELECT statement. The syntax of ORDER BY is:

```
SELECT columns
  FROM table
  ORDER BY
    sort_column1 [ASC | DESC],
    sort_column2 [ASC | DESC],
    ...
    sort_columnN [ASC | DESC];
```

columns is one or more comma-separated column names; *sort_column1*, *sort_column2*,..., *sort_columnN* are the names of the columns on which to sort the result; and *table* is the name of the table that contains *columns* and the sort columns. (The sort columns don't have to be in listed in *columns*.) Rows are sorted first by *sort_column1*; then rows that have equal values in *sort_column1* are sorted by the values in *sort_column2*, and so on. For each sort column, specify ASC for an ascending sort or DESC for a descending sort. If no sort direction is specified, ASC is assumed.

To list the authors' first names, last names, cities, and states, sorted by ascending last name, type:

```
SELECT au_fname, au_lname, city, state
  FROM authors
  ORDER BY au_lname ASC;
```

The result is:

```
au_fname  au_lname    city          state
--------- ----------- ------------- -----
Sarah     Buchman     Bronx         NY
Wendy     Heydemark   Boulder       CO
Hallie    Hull        San Francisco CA
Klee      Hull        San Francisco CA
Christian Kells       New York      NY
          Kellsey     Palo Alto     CA
Paddy     O'Furniture Sarasota      FL
```

Note that ORDER BY performs ascending sorts by default, so the ASC keyword is optional. To sort by descending last name, the DESC keyword is required:

```
SELECT au_fname, au_lname, city, state
  FROM authors
  ORDER BY au_lname DESC;
```

You can sort by multiple columns. To list the authors' first names, last names, cities, and states, sorted by descending city within ascending state, type:

```
SELECT au_fname, au_lname, city, state
  FROM authors
  ORDER BY
    state ASC,
    city  DESC;
```

The result is:

```
au_fname  au_lname    city          state
--------- ----------- ------------- -----
Hallie    Hull        San Francisco CA
Klee      Hull        San Francisco CA
          Kellsey     Palo Alto     CA
Wendy     Heydemark   Boulder       CO
Paddy     O'Furniture Sarasota      FL
Christian Kells       New York      NY
Sarah     Buchman     Bronx         NY
```

ORDER BY also lets you specify relative column-position numbers instead of column names. The position numbers refer to the columns in the result, not the original table. Using column positions saves typing, but the resulting code is unclear and invites mistakes if you reorder the columns in the SELECT clause.

The following statement lists each author's first name, last name, city, and state, sorted first by ascending state (column 4 in the SELECT clause) and then by descending last name within each state (column 2):

```
SELECT au_fname, au_lname, city, state
  FROM authors
  ORDER BY 4 ASC, 2 DESC;
```

The result is:

```
au_fname  au_lname    city          state
--------- ----------- ------------- -----
          Kellsey     Palo Alto     CA
Hallie    Hull        San Francisco CA
Klee      Hull        San Francisco CA
Wendy     Heydemark   Boulder       CO
Paddy     O'Furniture Sarasota      FL
Christian Kells       New York      NY
Sarah     Buchman     Bronx         NY
```

The column positions in the ORDER BY clause must be integers between 1 and the number of columns in the SELECT clause, inclusive. Each integer specifies the relative position of a column in the SELECT clause. (The sort numbers can't refer to a column that's not listed in the SELECT clause.)

Sorting Speed

The three factors that most affect sorting speed are, in order of importance:

- The number of rows selected
- The number of columns in the ORDER BY clause
- The length of columns in the ORDER BY clause

Always restrict a sort to the minimum number of rows needed. Running times of sorting routines don't scale linearly with the number of rows sorted—so sorting 10*n* rows takes much more than 10 times longer than sorting *n* rows. Also try to reduce the number of sorted columns and the columns' data-type lengths in the table definition, if possible.

Sort Order

Sorting numeric and datetime values is unambiguous; sorting character strings is complex. A DBMS uses a **collating sequence**, or **collation**, to determine the order in which characters are sorted. The collation defines the order of precedence for every character in your character set. Your character set depends on the language that you're using—European languages (a Latin character set), Hebrew (the Hebrew alphabet), or Chinese (ideographs), for example. The collation also determines case sensitivity (is 'A' < 'a'?), accent sensitivity (is 'A' < 'Á'?), width sensitivity (for multibyte or Unicode characters), and other factors such as linguistic practices. The SQL standard doesn't define particular collations and character sets, so each DBMS uses its own sorting strategy and default collation. DBMSs provide commands or tools that display the current collation and character set. Run the command `exec sp_helpsort` in **Microsoft SQL Server**, for example. Search your DBMS documentation for *collation* or *sort order*.

Tips for ORDER BY

- You can specify column aliases (page 28) instead of column names in ORDER BY.

- If the ORDER BY columns don't identify each row uniquely in the result, rows with duplicate values will be listed in arbitrary order. Although that's the case in some of the preceding examples, you should include enough ORDER BY columns to identify rows uniquely, particularly if the result is to be displayed to an end user.

- To sort based on conditional logic, add a CASE expression (Chapter 12) to the ORDER BY clause. For example, this query sorts by *price* if *type* is "history"; otherwise, it sorts by *sales*:

  ```
  SELECT title_id, type, price, sales
    FROM titles
    ORDER BY CASE WHEN type = 'history'
      THEN price ELSE sales END;
  ```

- You can sort by the results of expressions:

  ```
  SELECT
      title_id, price, sales,
      price * sales AS "Revenue"
    FROM titles
    ORDER BY "Revenue" DESC;
  ```

- You can intermingle column names, relative column positions, and expressions in ORDER BY.
- **DBMS** DBMSs restrict the columns that can appear in an ORDER BY clause, depending on data type. For example, in **Microsoft SQL Server**, you can't sort by ntext, text, and image columns; and in **Oracle**, you can't sort by blob, clob, nclob, and bfile columns. Search your DBMS documentation for *SELECT* or *ORDER BY*.

  In **Microsoft Access** you can't use an expression's column alias in ORDER BY. To run the preceding example, either retype the expression in the ORDER BY clause:

  ```
  ORDER BY price * sales DESC
  ```

  or use the relative column position:

  ```
  ORDER BY 4 DESC
  ```

Sorting and Nulls

Sorting is one of the situations where SQL departs from the idea that a null (page 22) isn't equal to any other value, including another null. (The logical comparison NULL = NULL is unknown, not true.) When nulls are sorted, they all are considered to be equal to one another. The SQL standard leaves it up to the DBMS to decide whether nulls are either greater than or less than all non-null values. **Microsoft Access**, **Microsoft SQL Server**, and **MySQL** treat nulls as the *lowest* possible values. **Oracle**, **DB2**, and **PostgreSQL** treat nulls as the *highest* possible values.

In **Oracle**, use NULLS FIRST or NULLS LAST with ORDER BY to control null-sorting behavior. For other DBMSs, create a derived column (page 64) that flags nulls—`CASE WHEN column IS NULL THEN 0 ELSE 1 END AS is_null`, for example—and add it as the first column (with ASC or DESC) in the ORDER BY clause.

Limiting the Number of Rows Returned

In practice it's common to use queries that return a certain number (*n*) of rows that fall at the top or the bottom of a range specified by an ORDER BY clause. SQL doesn't require an ORDER BY clause, but if you omit it, the query will return an arbitrary set of rows (because SQL doesn't promise to deliver query results in any particular order without an ORDER BY clause). The SQL code for limiting rows varies by DBMS.

Microsoft Access. To list the top three salespeople, including ties, type:

```
SELECT TOP 3 emp_id, sales
  FROM empsales
  ORDER BY sales DESC;
```

The result is:

```
emp_id sales
------ -----
E09      900
E02      800
E10      700
E05      700
```

The TOP clause always includes ties. Its syntax is:

```
TOP n [PERCENT]
```

To list the bottom 40 percent of salespeople, including ties, type:

```
SELECT TOP 40 PERCENT emp_id, sales
  FROM empsales
  ORDER BY sales ASC;
```

The result is:

```
emp_id sales
------ -----
E07      300
E08      400
E06      500
E04      500
E03      500
```

Microsoft SQL Server. To list the top three salespeople, not including ties, type:

```
SELECT TOP 3 emp_id, sales
  FROM empsales
  ORDER BY sales DESC;
```

The TOP clause's syntax is:

```
TOP n [PERCENT] [WITH TIES]
```

Oracle. The built-in ROWNUM pseudocolumn limits the number of rows returned. The first row selected has a ROWNUM of 1, the second has 2, and so on. To list the top three salespeople, not including ties, type:

```
SELECT emp_id, sales
  FROM (
    SELECT *
      FROM empsales
      ORDER BY sales DESC)
  WHERE ROWNUM <= 3;
```

IBM DB2. To list the top three salespeople, not including ties, type:

```
SELECT emp_id, sales
  FROM empsales
  ORDER BY sales DESC
  FETCH FIRST 3 ROWS ONLY;
```

The FETCH clause's syntax is:

```
FETCH FIRST n ROW[S] ONLY
```

MySQL and **PostgreSQL**. To list the top three salespeople, not including ties, type:

```
SELECT emp_id, sales
  FROM empsales
  ORDER BY sales DESC
  LIMIT 3;
```

The LIMIT clause's syntax is:

```
LIMIT n [OFFSET skip]
```

The OFFSET clause skips the specified number of initial rows. For example, LIMIT 3 OFFSET 5 return three rows starting from row 5.

CHAPTER 6

Filtering Rows

The WHERE Clause and Search Conditions

You can use the WHERE clause to filter unwanted rows from the result. This filtering capability gives the SELECT statement its real power. In a WHERE clause, you specify a **search condition** that has one or more conditions that need to be satisfied by the rows of a table. A **condition**, or **predicate**, is a logical expression that evaluates to true, false, or unknown. Rows for which the condition is true are included in the result; rows for which the condition is false or unknown are excluded. (An unknown result, which arises from nulls, is described in "True, False, and Unknown" on page 43.) SQL provides operators that express different types of conditions (Table 6.1). Operators are symbols or keywords that specify actions to perform on values or other elements.

Table 6.1 Types of Conditions

Condition	SQL Operators
Comparison	=, <>, <, <=, >, >= (this chapter)
Pattern matching	LIKE (Chapter 8)
Range filtering	BETWEEN (Chapter 9)
List filtering	IN (Chapter 9)
Null testing	IS NULL (Chapter 9)

Comparison Operators

SQL's **comparison operators** compare two values and evaluate to true, false, or unknown (Table 6.2). The data type determines how values are compared:

- Character strings are compared lexicographically. < means *precedes*, and > means *follows*.
- Numbers are compared arithmetically. < means *smaller*, and > means *larger*.
- Datetimes are compared chronologically. < means *earlier*, and > means *later*. Datetimes must have the same fields (year, month, day, hour, and so on) to be compared meaningfully.

Compare only identical or similar data types. If you try to compare values that have different data types, your DBMS might:

- Return an error

  or

- Compare the values unequally and return a result with no rows

  or

- Attempt to convert the values to a common type and compare them if successful or return an error if unsuccessful

Table 6.2 Comparison Operators

Operator	Description
=	Equal to
<>	Not equal to
<	Less than
<=	Less than or equal to
>	Greater than
>=	Greater than or equal to

Filtering Rows with WHERE

To filter rows by making a comparison, use a WHERE clause of the form:

```
WHERE test_column op value;
```

op is one of the comparison operators listed in Table 6.2, and *value* is a value that's compared with the value in *test_column*.

The right and left sides of the comparison can also be complex expressions. An expression (page 19) is any valid combination of column names, literals, functions, and operators that resolves to a single value (per row). The general form of a comparison is:

```
expression1 op expression2
```

To list the authors whose last name is not Hull, type:

```
SELECT au_id, au_fname, au_lname
  FROM authors
  WHERE au_lname <> 'Hull';
```

The result is:

```
au_id au_fname  au_lname
----- --------- -----------
A01   Sarah     Buchman
A02   Wendy     Heydemark
A05   Christian Kells
A06             Kellsey
A07   Paddy     O'Furniture
```

To list the titles for which there is no signed contract, type:

```
SELECT title_name, contract
  FROM titles
  WHERE contract = 0;
```

The result is:

```
title_name                 contract
-------------------------- --------
Not Without My Faberge Egg        0
```

To list the titles published in 2001 and later, type:

```
SELECT title_name, pubdate
  FROM titles
  WHERE pubdate >= DATE '2001-01-01';
```

The result is:

```
title_name                   pubdate
---------------------------- ----------
Exchange of Platitudes       2001-01-01
Just Wait Until After School 2001-06-01
Kiss My Boo-Boo              2002-05-31
```

To list the titles that generated more than $1 million in revenue, type:

```
SELECT
    title_name,
    price * sales AS "Revenue"
  FROM titles
  WHERE price * sales > 1000000;
```

The result is:

```
title_name                    Revenue
----------------------------- -----------
Ask Your System Administrator  1025396.65
Exchange of Platitudes         1400008.00
I Blame My Mother             35929790.00
Spontaneous, Not Annoying      1299012.99
```

DBMS Your DBMS's collation determines whether string comparisons are case insensitive ('A' = 'a') or case sensitive ('A' ≠ 'a'). **Microsoft Access**, **Microsoft SQL Server**, **DB2**, and **MySQL** perform case-insensitive comparisons by default. **Oracle** and **PostgreSQL** perform case-sensitive comparisons by default. In general, case-sensitive comparisons are slightly faster than case-insensitive ones.

In **Microsoft Access**, change the date in the example WHERE clause from `DATE '2001-01-01'` to `#2001-01-01#`. In **Microsoft SQL Server** and **DB2**, change the date to `'2001-01-01'`.

Some DBMSs support the comparison operator != as a synonym for <> (not equal). You should use <> to keep your code portable.

Comparisons and Nulls

A null (page 22) represents the unknown and won't match anything, not even another null. Rows in which nulls are involved in comparisons won't be in the result. To compare nulls, see "Testing for Nulls with IS NULL" on page 61.

CHAPTER 7

Combining and Negating Conditions

True, False, and Unknown

You can specify multiple conditions in a single WHERE clause to, say, retrieve rows based on the values in multiple columns. You can use the AND and OR operators to combine two or more conditions into a **compound condition**. AND, OR, and a third operator, NOT, are logical operators. **Logical operators**, or **Boolean operators**, are operators designed to work with **truth values**: true, false, and unknown.

If you've programmed in other languages (or studied propositional logic), you're familiar with the two-value logic (2VL) system. In **two-value logic**, the result of a logical expression is either true or false. 2VL assumes perfect knowledge, in which all propositions are known to be true or false. Databases model real data, however, and our knowledge of the world is imperfect—that's why we use nulls to represent unknown values (see "Nulls" on page 22).

2VL is insufficient to represent knowledge gaps, so SQL uses three-value logic (3VL). In **three-value logic**, the result of a logical expression is true, false, or unknown. If the result of a compound condition is false or unknown, the row is excluded from the result. (To retrieve rows with nulls, see "Testing for Nulls with IS NULL" on page 61.)

The AND Operator

The AND operator connects two conditions and returns true only if *both* conditions are true. Table 7.1 shows the possible outcomes when you combine two conditions with AND. The table's left column shows the truth values of the first condition, the top row shows the truth values of the second condition, and each intersection shows the AND outcome. This type of table is called a **truth table**.

Any number of conditions can be connected with multiple ANDs. All the conditions must be true for the row to be included in the result. AND is commutative: the order in which you list the conditions doesn't matter. You can enclose the conditions in parentheses to force the order in which they're evaluated.

To list the biographies that sell for less than $20, type:

```
SELECT title_name, type, price
  FROM titles
  WHERE type = 'biography' AND price < 20;
```

The result is:

```
title_name                type      price
------------------------- --------- -----
How About Never?          biography 19.95
Spontaneous, Not Annoying biography 12.99
```

To list the authors whose last names begin with one of the letters *H* through *Z* and who don't live in California, type:

```
SELECT au_fname, au_lname
  FROM authors
  WHERE au_lname >= 'H'
    AND au_lname <= 'Zz'
    AND state <> 'CA';
```

Table 7.1 AND Truth Table

AND	True	False	Unknown
True	True	False	Unknown
False	False	False	False
Unknown	Unknown	False	Unknown

The OR Operator

The OR operator connects two conditions and returns true if *either* condition is true or if *both* conditions are true. Table 7.2 shows the OR truth table.

Any number of conditions can be connected with multiple ORs. OR will retrieve rows that match any condition or all the conditions. As with AND, the order in which you list OR conditions doesn't matter, and can enclose the conditions in parentheses to force the order of evaluation.

To list the authors who live in New York State, Colorado, or San Francisco, type:

```
SELECT au_fname, au_lname, city, state
  FROM authors
  WHERE (state = 'NY')
     OR (state = 'CO')
     OR (city  = 'San Francisco');
```

The result is:

```
au_fname  au_lname  city          state
--------- --------- ------------- -----
Sarah     Buchman   Bronx         NY
Wendy     Heydemark Boulder       CO
Hallie    Hull      San Francisco CA
Klee      Hull      San Francisco CA
Christian Kells     New York      NY
```

Table 7.2 OR Truth Table

OR	True	False	Unknown
True	True	True	True
False	True	False	Unknown
Unknown	True	Unknown	Unknown

The NOT Operator

Unlike AND and OR, the NOT operator doesn't connect two conditions. Instead, it negates (reverses) a single condition. Table 7.3 shows the NOT truth table. To negate two or more conditions, repeat the NOT for each condition. To list titles that are not biographies and are not priced less than $20, for example, type:

```
SELECT title_id, type, price
  FROM titles
  WHERE NOT type = 'biography'
    AND NOT price < 20;      --Correct
```

and not:

```
SELECT title_id, type, price
  FROM titles
  WHERE NOT type = 'biography'
    AND price < 20;           --Wrong
```

To list the authors who don't live in California, type:

```
SELECT au_fname, au_lname, state
  FROM authors
  WHERE NOT (state = 'CA');
```

Tip: The clause `WHERE NOT state = 'CA'` is equivalent to `WHERE state <> 'CA'`.

You can enclose the condition in parentheses. To list the titles whose price is not less than $20 and that have sold more than 15000 copies, type:

```
SELECT title_name, sales, price
  FROM titles
  WHERE NOT (price < 20)
    AND (sales > 15000);
```

Table 7.3 NOT Truth Table

Condition	**NOT** *Condition*
True	False
False	True
Unknown	Unknown

Using AND, OR, and NOT Together

You can combine the three logical operators in a compound condition. Your DBMS uses SQL's precedence rules to determine which operators to evaluate first. Precedence is covered in "Determining the Order of Evaluation" on page 69, but for now you need know only that when you use multiple logical operators in a compound condition, NOT is evaluated first, then AND, and finally OR. You can override this order with parentheses: everything in parentheses is evaluated first. When parenthesized conditions are nested, the innermost condition is evaluated first. Under the default precedence rules, the condition

p AND NOT *q* OR *r*

is equivalent to

(*p* AND (NOT *q*)) OR *r*

It's wise to use parentheses, rather than rely on the default evaluation order, to make the evaluation order clear.

If I want to list history and biography titles priced less than $20, for example, this query won't work:

```
SELECT title_id, type, price
  FROM titles
  WHERE type  = 'history'
     OR type  = 'biography'
    AND price < 20;
```

AND is evaluated before OR, so the query is evaluated as follows:

1 Find all the biography titles less than $20.

2 Find all the history titles (regardless of price).

3 List both sets of titles in the result.

The result is:

```
title_id type      price
-------- --------- -----
T01      history   21.99
T02      history   19.95
T06      biography 19.95
T12      biography 12.99
T13      history   29.99
```

To fix the preceding query, add parentheses to force evaluation of OR first:

```
SELECT title_id, type, price
  FROM titles
  WHERE (type  = 'history'
     OR  type  = 'biography')
    AND  price < 20;
```

1 Find all the biography and history titles.

2 Of the titles found in step 1, keep the ones priced less than $20.

3 List the subset of titles in the result.

The result is:

```
title_id type      price
-------- --------- -----
T02      history   19.95
T06      biography 19.95
T12      biography 12.99
```

Column Aliases and WHERE

If you alias a column in a SELECT clause (page 28), you can't reference it in the WHERE clause. The following query fails because the WHERE clause is evaluated before the SELECT clause, so the alias *copies_sold* doesn't yet exist when the WHERE clause is evaluated:

```
-- Wrong
SELECT sales AS copies_sold
  FROM titles
  WHERE copies_sold > 100000;
```

Instead, use a subquery (Chapter 17) in the FROM clause, which is evaluated before the WHERE clause:

```
-- Correct
SELECT *
  FROM (SELECT sales AS copies_sold
          FROM titles) ta
  WHERE copies_sold > 100000;
```

This solution works not only for columns aliases but also for aggregate functions, scalar subqueries, and windowing functions referenced in WHERE clauses. Note that in the latter query, the subquery is aliased *ta* (a table alias). All DBMSs accept table aliases, but not all require them.

Tips for AND, OR, and NOT

- If your search condition contains only AND operators, your query will run faster if you put the conditions *least* likely to be true first. If *col1='A'* is less likely than *col2='B'* then

  ```
  WHERE col1 = 'A' AND col2 = 'B'
  ```

  is faster than

  ```
  WHERE col2 = 'B' AND col1 = 'A'
  ```

  because the DBMS won't bother to evaluate the second expression if the first is false. For search conditions that contain only OR operators, do the reverse: put the *most* likely conditions first. If the conditions are equally likely, put the least complex expression first.

  This logic depends on your DBMS's optimizer reading WHERE clauses from left to right, which most do. **Oracle**'s cost-based optimizer (as opposed to its rule-based optimizer), however, reads right to left.

- Table 7.4 shows alternative ways of expressing the same condition. The first equivalency is **double negation**, the second two are **De Morgan's Laws**, and the final two are the **distributive laws**.

- Some DBMSs support the **exclusive-or** (or **XOR**) logical operator, which yields true only if exactly one of its operands is true:

  p XOR *q*

  is equivalent to

  (*p* AND (NOT *q*)) OR ((NOT *p*) AND *q*)

- **DBMS** In **MySQL** 4.0.4 and earlier, false AND unknown evaluates to unknown, not false.

Table 7.4 Equivalent Conditions

This Condition	Is Equivalent To
NOT (NOT *p*)	*p*
NOT (*p* AND *q*)	(NOT *p*) OR (NOT *q*)
NOT (*p* OR *q*)	(NOT *p*) AND (NOT *q*)
p AND (*q* OR *r*)	(*p* AND *q*) OR (*p* AND *r*)
p OR (*q* AND *r*)	(*p* OR *q*) AND (*p* OR *r*)

Re-expressing Conditions

You must master the laws in Table 7.4 to become a competent programmer in SQL (or any language). They're especially useful when you want to re-express conditions to make queries run faster. For example, the statement

```
SELECT * FROM mytable
  WHERE col1 = 1
    AND NOT (col1 = col2 OR col3 = 3);
```

is equivalent to

```
SELECT * FROM mytable
  WHERE col1 = 1
    AND col2 <> 1
    AND col3 <> 3;
```

but the latter one will run faster if your DBMS's optimizer isn't smart enough to re-express the former internally. (The condition *col1 = col2* is more expensive computationally than comparing *col1* and *col2* to literal values.)

You also can use the laws to change a condition into its opposite. For example, the reverse of the condition

```
WHERE (col1 = 'A') AND (col2 = 'B')
```

is

```
WHERE (col1 <> 'A') OR (col2 <> 'B')
```

In this case, it would have easier just to negate the entire original expression with NOT:

```
WHERE NOT ((col1 = 'A') AND (col2 = 'B'))
```

But this simple approach won't work with complex conditions involving multiple ANDs, ORs, and NOTs.

Here's a problem to solve: look at only the first code line below and see whether you can repeatedly apply equivalency rules to push the NOT operators inward until they apply to only the individual expressions *p*, *q*, and *r*:

```
NOT ((p AND q) OR (NOT p AND r))
= NOT (p AND q) AND NOT (NOT p AND r)
= (NOT p OR NOT q) AND (p OR NOT r)
```

CHAPTER 8

Pattern Matching

Matching Patterns with LIKE

The preceding examples retrieved rows based on the exact value of a column or columns. You can use LIKE to retrieve rows based on partial information. LIKE is useful if you don't know an exact value ("The author's last name is *Kel*-something") or you want to retrieve rows with similar values ("Which authors live in the San Francisco Bay Area?").

- LIKE works with only character strings, not numbers or datetimes.
- LIKE uses a pattern that values are matched against. A **pattern** is a quoted string that contains the literal characters to match and any combination of wildcards. **Wildcards** are special characters used to match parts of a value. Table 8.1 lists the wildcard operators, and Table 8.2 lists some example patterns.
- String comparisons are case insensitive or case sensitive, depending on your DBMS.
- You can negate a LIKE condition with NOT LIKE.
- You can combine LIKE conditions and other conditions with AND and OR (Chapter 7).

Tip: Wildcard searches are time-consuming—particularly if you use % at the start of a pattern. Don't use wildcards if another type of search will do.

To filter rows by matching a pattern, use a WHERE clause of the form:

```
WHERE test_column [NOT] LIKE 'pattern'
```

pattern is the pattern that's compared with the value in *test_column*. *pattern* is a string like one of the examples listed in Table 8.2. To retrieve rows with values that don't match *pattern*, specify NOT LIKE.

Table 8.1 Wildcard Operators

Operator	Matches
%	A percent sign matches any string of zero or more characters.
_	An underscore matches any one character.

Table 8.2 Examples of % and _ Patterns

Pattern	Matches
'A%'	Matches a string of length ≥ 1 that begins with *A*, including the single letter *A*. Matches 'A', 'Anonymous', and 'AC/DC'.
'%s'	Matches a string of length ≥ 1 that ends with *s*, including the single letter *s*. A string with trailing spaces (after the *s*) won't match. Matches 's', 'Victoria Falls', and 'DBMSs'.
'%in%'	Matches a string of length ≥ 2 that contains *in* anywhere. Matches 'in', 'inch', 'Pine', 'linchpin', and 'lynchpin'.
'____'	Matches any four-character string. Matches 'ABCD', 'I am', and 'Jack'.
'Qua__'	Matches any five-character string that begins with *Qua*. Matches 'Quack', 'Quaff', and 'Quake'.
'_re_'	Matches any four-character string that has *re* as its second and third characters. Matches 'Tree', 'area', and 'fret'.
'_re%'	Matches a string of length ≥ 3 that begins with any character and has *re* as its second and third characters. Matches 'Tree', 'area', 'fret', 'are', and 'fretful'.
'%re_'	Matches a string of length ≥ 3 that has *re* as the second and third characters from its end and ends with any character. Matches 'Tree', 'area', 'fret', 'red', and 'Blood red'.

To list the authors whose last names begin with *Kel*, type:

```
SELECT au_fname, au_lname
  FROM authors
  WHERE au_lname LIKE 'Kel%';
```

The result is:

```
au_fname  au_lname
--------- --------
Christian Kells
          Kellsey
```

To list the authors whose last names have *ll* (el-el) as the third and fourth characters, type:

```
SELECT au_fname, au_lname
  FROM authors
  WHERE au_lname LIKE '__ll%';
```

The result is:

```
au_fname  au_lname
--------- --------
Hallie    Hull
Klee      Hull
Christian Kells
          Kellsey
```

To list the authors who live in the San Francisco Bay Area (that is, with postal codes that begin with *94*), type:

```
SELECT au_fname, au_lname, city, state, zip
  FROM authors
  WHERE zip LIKE '94___';
```

The result is:

```
au_fname au_lname city          state zip
-------- -------- ------------- ----- -----
Hallie   Hull     San Francisco CA    94123
Klee     Hull     San Francisco CA    94123
         Kellsey  Palo Alto     CA    94305
```

The following query lists the authors who live outside the 212, 415, and 303 area codes. This example shows three alternative patterns for excluding telephone numbers. You should favor the first alternative because single-character matches (_) are faster than multiple-character ones (%).

```
SELECT au_fname, au_lname, phone
  FROM authors
  WHERE phone NOT LIKE '212-___-____'
    AND phone NOT LIKE '415-___-%'
    AND phone NOT LIKE '303-%';
```

The result is:

```
au_fname au_lname    phone
-------- ----------- ------------
Sarah    Buchman     718-496-7223
         Kellsey     650-836-7128
Paddy    O'Furniture 941-925-0752
```

Escape Characters

You can search for values that contain the special wildcard characters. Use the ESCAPE keyword to specify an escape character that you can use to search for a percent sign or underscore as a literal character. Immediately precede a wildcard character with an escape character to strip the wild-card of its special meaning. If the escape character is !, for example, !% in a pattern searches values for a literal %. (Unescaped wildcards still have their special meaning.) The escape character can't be part of the value that you're trying to retrieve; if you're searching for '50% OFF!', choose an escape character other than !. Table 8.3 shows some examples of escaped and unescaped patterns; the designated escape character is !.

Table 8.3 Escaped and Unescaped Patterns

Pattern	Matches
'100%'	Unescaped. Matches *100* followed by a string of zero or more characters.
'100!%'	Escaped. Matches '100%'.
'_op'	Unescaped. Matches 'top', 'hop', 'pop', and so on.
'!_op'	Escaped. Matches '_op'.

To match a wildcard character, use a WHERE clause of the form:

```
WHERE test_column [NOT] LIKE 'pattern' ESCAPE 'escape_char'
```

escape_char is a single character. Any character in *pattern* that follows *escape_char* is interpreted literally; *escape_char* itself is not considered to be part of the search pattern.

The following query lists the titles that contain percent signs. Only the % that follows the escape character ! has its literal meaning; the other two percent signs still act as wildcards.

```
SELECT title_name
  FROM titles
  WHERE title_name LIKE '%!%%' ESCAPE '!';
```

No title names contain a % character, so the result is empty:

```
title_name
----------------------------------------
```

Tips for LIKE

- The NOT that can precede LIKE is independent of the NOT that can precede *test_column* (see "The NOT Operator" on page 46). The clause

  ```
  WHERE phone NOT LIKE '212-%'
  ```

  is equivalent to

  ```
  WHERE NOT phone LIKE '212-%'
  ```

  You even can write this silly double negation, which retrieves everyone with a 212 area code:

  ```
  WHERE NOT phone NOT LIKE '212-%'
  ```

- In the simplest case in which a pattern contains no wildcards, LIKE works like an = comparison (and NOT LIKE works like <>). In many cases

  ```
  WHERE city LIKE 'New York'
  ```

  is equivalent to

  ```
  WHERE city = 'New York'
  ```

  But these comparisons will differ if your DBMS takes trailing spaces into account for LIKE but not for =. If that's not important, the = form is usually faster than LIKE.

- **DBMS** **Microsoft Access** doesn't support the ESCAPE clause. Instead, surround a wildcard character with brackets to render it a literal character. Replace the WHERE clause in the ESCAPE example above with:

```
WHERE title_name LIKE '%[%]%'
```

Some DBMSs let you use **regular expressions** to match patterns. **Microsoft SQL Server**, for example, supports a limited variant of POSIX-style regular expressions. The [] wildcard matches any single character within a range or set, and the [^] wildcard matches any single character *not* within a range or set. Table 8.4 lists some examples. The SQL standard uses the SIMILAR operator for regex matching. Regex support varies by DBMS; search your DBMS documentation for *LIKE*, *regular expressions*, or *pattern matching*.

Some DBMSs let you use LIKE to search numeric and datetime columns.

Table 8.4 Examples of [] and [^] Patterns

Pattern	Matches
'[a-c]at'	Matches 'bat' and 'cat' but not 'fat'.
'[bcf]at'	Matches 'bat', 'cat', and 'fat' but not 'eat'.
'[^c]at'	Matches 'bat' and 'fat' but not 'cat'.
'se[^n]%'	Matches strings of length ≥ 2 that begin with *se* and whose third character isn't *n*.

CHAPTER 9

More Ways to Filter Rows

Range Filtering with BETWEEN

BETWEEN determines whether a given value falls within a specified range (a low value and a high value).

- BETWEEN works with character strings, numbers, and datetimes.
- BETWEEN is a convenient, shorthand clause that you can replicate by using AND.

  ```
  WHERE test_column BETWEEN low_value AND high_value
  ```

  is equivalent to:

  ```
  WHERE (test_column >= low_value)
    AND (test_column <= high_value)
  ```

- BETWEEN specifies an **inclusive range**, in which the high value and low value are included in the search. To specify an **exclusive range**, which excludes endpoints, use > and < comparisons instead of BETWEEN:

  ```
  WHERE (test_column > low_value)
    AND (test_column < high_value)
  ```

- String comparisons are case insensitive or case sensitive, depending on your DBMS.
- You can negate a BETWEEN condition with NOT BETWEEN.
- You can combine BETWEEN conditions and other conditions with AND and OR (Chapter 7).

To filter rows by using a range, use a WHERE clause of the form:

```
WHERE test_column [NOT] BETWEEN low_value AND high_value
```

low_value and *high_value* specify the endpoints of the range that is compared with the value in *test_column*. *low_value* must be less than or equal to *high_value*, and both values must be the same as or comparable to the data type of *test_column*. To match values that lie outside the range, specify NOT BETWEEN.

To list the authors who live outside the postal range 20000–89999, type:

```
SELECT au_fname, au_lname, zip
  FROM authors
  WHERE zip NOT BETWEEN '20000' AND '89999';
```

The result is:

```
au_fname  au_lname zip
--------- -------- -----
Sarah     Buchman  10468
Hallie    Hull     94123
Klee      Hull     94123
Christian Kells    10014
          Kellsey  94305
```

To list the titles priced between $10 and $19.95, inclusive, type:

```
SELECT title_id, price
  FROM titles
  WHERE price BETWEEN 10 AND 19.95;
```

The result is:

```
title_id price
-------- -----
T02      19.95
T04      12.99
T06      19.95
T08      10.00
T09      13.95
T12      12.99
```

Tips for BETWEEN

- The NOT that can precede BETWEEN is independent of the NOT that can precede *test_column*; see "Tips for LIKE" on page 55.

- To rewrite the preceding example with an exclusive range, which doesn't include the $10 and $19.95 endpoints, type:

```
SELECT title_id, price
  FROM titles
  WHERE (price > 10)
    AND (price < 19.95);
```

- Specifying a character range often needs some thought. Suppose you want to search for last names that begin with the letter *F*. The following clause won't work because it will retrieve someone whose last name is the letter *G* (*is* the letter *G*, not *starts* with the letter *G*):

```
WHERE last_name BETWEEN 'F' AND 'G'
```

  This next clause shows the correct way to specify the ending point (in most cases):

```
WHERE last_name BETWEEN 'F' AND 'Fz'
```

- **DBMS** In some DBMSs, *low_value* can exceed *high_value*; search your DBMS documentation for *WHERE* or *BETWEEN*.

List Filtering with IN

IN determines whether a given value matches any value in a specified list.

- IN works with character strings, numbers, and datetimes.
- The IN list is a parenthesized listing of one or more comma-separated values. The list items needn't be in any particular order.
- IN is a convenient, shorthand clause that you can replicate by using OR.

```
WHERE test_column IN
      (value1, value2, value3)
```

  is equivalent to:

```
WHERE (test_column = value1)
   OR (test_column = value2)
   OR (test_column = value3)
```

- String comparisons are case insensitive or case sensitive, depending on your DBMS.
- You can negate an IN condition with NOT IN.
- You can combine IN conditions and other conditions with AND and OR (Chapter 7).

To filter rows by using a list, use a WHERE clause of the form:

```
WHERE test_column [NOT] IN (value1, value2,...)
```

value1, *value2*,... are one or more comma-separated values that are compared with the value in *test_column*. The list values can appear in any order and must be the same as or comparable to the data type of *test_column*. To match values that aren't in the list, specify NOT IN.

To list the authors who don't live in New York State, New Jersey, or California, type:

```
SELECT au_fname, au_lname, state
  FROM authors
  WHERE state NOT IN ('NY', 'NJ', 'CA');
```

The result is:

```
au_fname au_lname    state
-------- ----------- -----
Wendy    Heydemark   CO
Paddy    O'Furniture FL
```

To list the titles for which advances of $0, $1000, or $5000 were paid, type:

```
SELECT title_id, advance
  FROM royalties
  WHERE advance IN (0.00, 1000.00, 5000.00);
```

The result is:

```
title_id advance
-------- -------
T02      1000.00
T08         0.00
T09         0.00
```

Tips for IN

- The NOT that can precede IN is independent of the NOT that can precede *test_column*; see "Tips for LIKE" on page 55.
- If your list contains a large number of values, your code will be easier to read if you use one IN condition instead of many OR conditions. (Also, one IN usually runs faster than multiple ORs.)
- For speed, list the most likely values first. If you're testing U.S. addresses, for example, list the most populous states first:

  ```
  WHERE state IN ('CA', 'TX', 'NY', 'FL',...,'DC', 'WY')
  ```

- The search condition

  ```
  WHERE col1 BETWEEN 1 AND 5
    AND col1 <> 3
  ```

  usually is faster than

  ```
  WHERE col1 IN (1, 2, 4, 5)
  ```

- A compound condition's order of evaluation is easier to read and manage if you use IN instead of multiple ORs.
- You also can use IN to determine whether a given value matches any value in a subquery (Chapter 17).
- NOT IN is equivalent to combining tests for inequality with AND. This statement is equivalent to the first IN example:

  ```
  SELECT au_fname, au_lname, state
    FROM authors
    WHERE state <> 'NY'
      AND state <> 'NJ'
      AND state <> 'CA';
  ```

Testing for Nulls with IS NULL

Recall that nulls (page 22) represent missing or unknown values. This situation causes a problem: LIKE, BETWEEN, IN, and other WHERE-clause conditions can't find nulls because unknown values don't satisfy specific conditions. A null matches no value—not even other nulls. You can't use = or <> to test whether a value is null. Fortunately, SQL provides IS NULL to determine whether a given value is null.

- IS NULL works for columns of any data type.
- You can negate an IS NULL condition with IS NOT NULL.
- You can combine IS NULL conditions and other conditions with AND and OR (Chapter 7).

To retrieve rows with nulls or non-null values, use a WHERE clause of the form:

```
WHERE test_column IS [NOT] NULL;
```

To match non-null values, specify NOT NULL.

To list the publishers located outside California, type:

```
SELECT pub_id, city, state, country
  FROM publishers
  WHERE state <> 'CA'
     OR state IS NULL;
```

The result is:

```
pub_id city     state country
------ -------- ----- -------
P01    New York NY    USA
P03    Hamburg  NULL  Germany
```

To list the biographies whose (past or future) publication dates are known, type:

```
SELECT title_id, type, pubdate
  FROM titles
  WHERE type = 'biography'
    AND pubdate IS NOT NULL;
```

Tips for IS NULL

- The NOT that can precede NULL is independent of the NOT that can precede *test_column*; see “Tips for LIKE” on page 55.
- Nulls cause rows to be excluded from results only if a column containing nulls is a test column in a WHERE condition. The following query, for example, retrieves all the rows in the table *publishers* because the null in the column *state* isn't compared with anything:

  ```
  SELECT pub_id, city, state, country
    FROM publishers
    WHERE country <> 'Canada';
  ```

- It bears repeating that a null isn't the same as an empty string (''). In the table *authors*, for example, the column *au_fname* contains an empty string for author A06 (last name of Kellsey). The WHERE condition to find the first name is

  ```
  WHERE au_fname = ''
  ```

  and not

  ```
  WHERE au_fname IS NULL
  ```

- **DBMS** **Oracle** treats an empty string ('') as a null; see the DBMS tip in “Tips for nulls” on page 23.

CHAPTER 10

Operators and Functions

Understanding Operators and Functions

Operators and functions let you calculate results derived from column values, system-determined values, constants, and other data. You can perform:

- Arithmetic operations—Cut everyone's salary by 10 percent.
- String operations—Concatenate personal information into a mailing address.
- Datetime operations—Compute the time interval between two dates.
- System operations—Find out what time your DBMS thinks it is.

An **operator** is a symbol or keyword indicating an operation that acts on one or more elements. The elements, called **operands**, are SQL expressions. An expression (page 19) is any legal combination of symbols and tokens that evaluates to a single value (or null). In the expression *price * 2*, for example, * is the operator, and *price* and *2* are its operands.

A **function** is a built-in, named routine that performs a specialized task. Most functions take parenthesized **arguments**, which are values you pass to the function that the function then uses to perform its task. Arguments can be column names, literals, nested functions, or more-complex expressions. In *TRIM(au_lname)*, for example, *TRIM* is the function name, and *au_lname* is the argument.

Creating Derived Columns

You can use operators and functions to create derived columns. A **derived column** is the result of a calculation and is created with a SELECT-clause expression that is something other than a simple reference to a column. Derived columns don't become permanent columns in a table; they're for display and reporting purposes.

The values in a derived column are often computed from values in existing columns, but you can also create a derived column by using a constant expression (such as a string, number, or date) or system value (such as the system time). The following SELECT statement yields a trivial arithmetic calculation; it needs no FROM clause because it doesn't retrieve data from a table.

```
SELECT 2 + 3;
```

The result is:

```
2 + 3
-----
    5
```

Closure (page 9) guarantees that every result is a table, so even this simple result is a table: a 1 × 1 table that contains the value 5. If I retrieve a column along with a constant, the constant appears in every row of the result:

```
SELECT au_id, 2 + 3
  FROM authors;
```

The result is:

```
au_id 2 + 3
----- -----
A01       5
A02       5
A03       5
A04       5
A05       5
A06       5
A07       5
```

Your DBMS will assign the derived column a default name, typically the expression itself as a quoted identifier. You should name derived columns explicitly with an AS clause (page 28) because system-assigned names can be long, unwieldy, and inconvenient for database applications to refer to.

In the following query, the two derived columns would have DBMS-specific default names if the AS clauses were removed:

```
SELECT
    title_id,
    price,
    0.10 AS "Discount",
    price * (1 - 0.10) AS "New price"
  FROM titles;
```

The result (shortened for brevity) is:

```
title_id price Discount New price
-------- ----- -------- ---------
T01      21.99     0.10     19.79
T02      19.95     0.10     17.95
T03      39.95     0.10     35.96
...
```

Tips for derived columns

- **DBMS** **Oracle** requires a FROM clause in a SELECT statement and so creates the **dummy table** DUAL automatically to be used for SELECTing a constant expression; search Oracle documentation for *DUAL table*. To run the first example query, add a FROM clause that selects the constant value from DUAL:

  ```
  SELECT 2 + 3
    FROM DUAL;
  ```

  DB2 requires a FROM clause in a SELECT statement and so creates the dummy table SYSIBM.SYSDUMMY1 automatically to be used for SELECTing a constant expression; search DB2 documentation for *SYSIBM.SYSDUMMY1*. To run the first example query, add a FROM clause that selects the constant value from SYSIBM.SYSDUMMY1:

  ```
  SELECT 2 + 3
    FROM SYSIBM.SYSDUMMY1;
  ```

Performing Arithmetic Operations

A **monadic** (or **unary**) **arithmetic operator** performs a mathematical operation on a single numeric operand to produce a result. The - (negation) operator changes the sign of its operand, and the not-very-useful + (identity) operator leaves its operand unchanged. A **dyadic** (or **binary**) **arithmetic operator** performs a mathematical operation on two numeric operands to produce a result. These operators include the usual ones: + (addition), - (subtraction), * (multiplication), and / (division). Table 10.1 lists SQL's arithmetic operators (*expr* is a numeric expression).

In the following query, the negation operator changes the sign of a number:

```
SELECT
    title_id,
    -advance AS "Advance"
  FROM royalties;
```

The result (shortened for brevity) is:

```
title_id Advance
-------- -----------
T01        -10000.00
T02         -1000.00
T03        -15000.00
T04        -20000.00
T05       -100000.00
T06        -20000.00
T07      -1000000.00
T08            0.00
...
```

Table 10.1 Arithmetic Operators

Operator	What It Does
-expr	Reverses the sign of *expr*
+expr	Leaves *expr* unchanged
expr1 + expr2	Sums *expr1* and *expr2*
expr1 - expr2	Subtracts *expr2* from *expr1*
*expr1 * expr2*	Multiplies *expr1* and *expr2*
expr1 / expr2	Divides *expr1* by *expr2*

To list the biographies by descending revenue (= price × sales), type:

```
SELECT
    title_id,
    price * sales AS "Revenue"
  FROM titles
  WHERE type = 'biography'
  ORDER BY price * sales DESC;
```

The result is:

```
title_id Revenue
-------- -----------
T07       35929790.00
T12        1299012.99
T06         225834.00
T10              NULL
```

Tips for arithmetic operations

- The result of any arithmetic operation that involves a null is null (page 22).
- If you use multiple operators in a single expression, you may need to use parentheses to control the calculation order (page 69).
- If you mix numeric data types in an arithmetic expression, your DBMS converts, or **coerces**, all the numbers to the data type of the expression's most complex operand and returns the result in this type. This conversion process is called **promotion**. If you add an INTEGER and a FLOAT, for example, the DBMS converts the integer to a float, adds the numbers, and returns the sum as a float. In some cases, you must convert a data type to another data type explicitly (see "Converting Data Types" on page 77).
- If you're writing a database application or UPDATEing rows, note that data types aren't **closed** for some arithmetic operations. If you multiply or add two SMALLINTs, for example, the result might be greater than a SMALLINT column can hold. Similarly, dividing two INTEGERs doesn't necessarily yield an INTEGER (page 68).

Integer Truncation

DBMS Sometimes DBMSs force mathematical closure, so be careful when dividing integers by integers. If an integer dividend is divided by an integer divisor, the result may be an integer that has any fractional part of the result truncated. In the example below, you might expect the two derived columns to contain the same values, because the column *pages* (an INTEGER) is divided by two equal constants: 10 (an integer) and 10.0 (a float). **Microsoft Access**, **Oracle**, and **MySQL** return the result you'd expect (Result 1), but **Microsoft SQL Server**, **DB2**, and **PostgreSQL** truncate the result of an integer division (Result 2).

In the following query, the first derived column divides *pages* by the integer constant 10, and the second derived column divides *pages* by the floating-point constant 10.0. In the result, you'd expect identical values to be in both derived columns.

```
SELECT
    title_id,
    pages,
    pages/10   AS "pages/10",
    pages/10.0 AS "pages/10.0"
  FROM titles;
```

Result 1 (shortened for brevity)—In Microsoft Access, Oracle, and MySQL, dividing two integers yields a floating-point number (as you'd expect):

```
title_id pages pages/10 pages/10.0
-------- ----- -------- ----------
T01        107     10.7       10.7
T02         14      1.4        1.4
T03       1226    122.6      122.6
T04        510     51.0       51.0
...
```

Result 2 (shortened for brevity)—In Microsoft SQL Server, DB2, and PostgreSQL, dividing two integers yields an integer; the fractional part of the result is discarded (not as you'd expect):

```
title_id pages pages/10 pages/10.0
-------- ----- -------- ----------
T01        107       10       10.7
T02         14        1        1.4
T03       1226      122      122.6
T04        510       51       51.0
...
```

Determining the Order of Evaluation

Precedence determines the priority of various operators when more than one operator is used in an expression. Operators with higher precedence are evaluated first. Arithmetic operators (+, -, *, and so on) have higher precedence than comparison operators (<, =, >, and so on), which have higher precedence than logical operators (NOT, AND, OR), so the expression

a or b * c >= d

is equivalent to

a or ((b * c) >= d)

Operators with lower precedence are less **binding** than those with higher precedence. Table 10.2 lists operator precedences from most to least binding. Operators in the same row have equal precedence.

Table 10.2 Order of Evaluation (Highest to Lowest)

Operator	Description
+, -	Monadic identity, monadic negation
*, /	Multiplication, division
+, -	Addition, subtraction
=, <>, <, <=, >, >=	Comparison operators
NOT	Logical NOT
AND	Logical AND
OR	Logical OR

Other Operators and Functions

All DBMSs provide plenty of operators and functions in addition to those defined in the SQL standard (or covered in this book). In fact, the standard is playing catch-up—many of the functions introduced in the latest standard have existed for years in DBMSs. The earlier standards were so anemic that they left SQL weaker than a desktop calculator. If you search your DBMS documentation for *operators* and *functions*, you'll find mathematical, statistical, financial, scientific, trigonometric, conversion, string, datetime, bitwise, system, metadata, security, and other categories.

Associativity determines the order of evaluation in an expression when adjacent operators have equal precedence. SQL uses left-to-right associativity.

You don't need to memorize all this information. You can use parentheses to override precedence and associativity rules. In the following query, the first and second columns show how to use parentheses to override precedence rules. The third and fourth columns show how to use parentheses to override associativity rules:

```
SELECT
    2 + 3 * 4   AS "2+3*4",
    (2 + 3) * 4 AS "(2+3)*4",
    6 / 2 * 3   AS "6/2*3",
    6 / (2 * 3) AS "6/(2*3)";
```

The result is:

```
2+3*4 (2+3)*4 6/2*3 6/(2*3)
----- ------- ----- -------
   14      20     9       1
```

Tips for order of evaluation

- It's good programming style to add parentheses (even when they're unnecessary) to complex expressions to ensure your intended evaluation order and make code more portable and easier to read.
- **DBMS** Table 10.2 is incomplete; it omits some standard (such as IN and EXISTS) and nonstandard (DBMS-specific) operators. To determine the complete order of evaluation that your DBMS uses, search your DBMS documentation for *precedence*.

  To run the preceding query in **Oracle**, add the clause `FROM DUAL`. To run it in **DB2**, add the clause `FROM SYSIBM.SYSDUMMY1`. See the DBMS tip in "Tips for derived columns" on page 65.

CHAPTER 11

Working with Functions

Concatenating Strings

The || operator combines, or **concatenates**, strings.

- The operator || is two consecutive vertical-bar, or pipe, characters.
- Concatenation doesn't add a space between strings.
- You can chain concatenations to combine multiple strings into a single string: 'a' || 'b' || 'c' || 'd' is 'abcd'.
- Concatenation with an empty string ('') leaves a string unchanged: 'a' || '' || 'b' is 'ab'.
- The result of any concatenation operation that involves a null is null: 'a' || NULL || 'b' is NULL. (But see the **Oracle** exception below.)
- To concatenate a string and a nonstring (such as a numeric or date time value), you must use CAST() to convert the nonstring to a string if your DBMS doesn't convert it implicitly (see "Converting Data Types" on page 77).

To list the authors' first and last names, concatenated into a single column and sorted by last name/first name, type:

```
SELECT au_fname || ' ' || au_lname
    AS "Author name"
  FROM authors
  ORDER BY au_lname ASC, au_fname ASC;
```

The result is:

```
Author name
-----------------
Sarah Buchman
Wendy Heydemark
Hallie Hull
Klee Hull
Christian Kells
 Kellsey
Paddy O'Furniture
```

Tip: To remove unwanted spaces from concatenated strings, use the TRIM() function. CHARACTER values (page 238) are padded with trailing spaces, sometimes creating long, ugly stretches of spaces in concatenated strings. To remove the extra space in front of the name *Kellsey* in the preceding result, for example, type TRIM(au_fname || ' ' || au_lname).

DBMS In **Microsoft Access** and **Microsoft SQL Server**, the concatenation operator is +. To run the preceding query, change the concatenation expression to:

```
au_fname + ' ' + au_lname
```

In **MySQL**, the concatenation function is CONCAT(). The || operator is legal, but it means logical OR in MySQL by default. (Use PIPES_AS_CONCAT mode to treat || as a string-concatenation operator rather than as a synonym for OR.) CONCAT() takes any number of arguments and converts nonstrings to strings as necessary (so CAST() isn't needed). To run the preceding query, change the concatenation expression to:

```
CONCAT(au_fname, ' ', au_lname)
```

For string operations, **Oracle** treats a null as an empty string: 'a' || NULL || 'b' returns 'ab' (not NULL). See the DBMS tip in "Tips for nulls" on page 23.

Oracle and **DB2** also support the CONCAT() function.

Trimming Spaces from Strings

The function TRIM() removes unwanted spaces from the ends of a string.

- You can trim leading spaces, trailing spaces, or both. (You can't use TRIM() to remove spaces from *within* a string.)
- TRIM() typically is used to format results and make comparisons in a WHERE clause.

- TRIM() is useful for trimming trailing spaces from CHARACTER values (page 238). DBMSs add spaces automatically to the end of CHARACTER values to create strings of exactly a specified length.
- Trimming has no effect on empty strings ('').
- If any argument is null, TRIM() returns null. (But see the **Oracle** exception below.

Tip: By default, TRIM() trims spaces, but you can strip off any unwanted characters, such as leading and trailing zeros or asterisks, by using TRIM() and DBMS-specific functions. Search your DBMS documentation for *character functions* or *string functions*.

To trim spaces from a string, type the function:

```
TRIM([[LEADING | TRAILING | BOTH] FROM] string)
```

Specify LEADING to remove leading spaces, TRAILING to remove trailing spaces, or BOTH (the default) to remove leading and trailing spaces.

To list the three-character title IDs that start with T1, ignoring leading and trailing spaces, type:

```
SELECT title_id
  FROM titles
  WHERE TRIM(title_id) LIKE 'T1_';
```

The result is:

```
title_id
--------
T10
T11
T12
T13
```

DBMS In **Microsoft Access**, **Microsoft SQL Server**, and **DB2** the trimming functions are LTRIM(*string*) to trim leading spaces, RTRIM(*string*) to trailing spaces. Access also supports TRIM(*string*). To run the preceding query, change the trim expression to:

```
LTRIM(RTRIM(title_id)) LIKE 'T1_'
```

For string operations, **Oracle** treats a null as an empty string: TRIM(NULL) returns '' (not NULL). See the DBMS tip in "Tips for nulls" on page 23.

Other String Functions

String functions are some of the most frequently used functions in SQL programming. Search your DBMS documentation for *character functions* or *string functions* to find functions that, for example,

- Extract part of a string (called a substring)
- Convert strings to lowercase or uppercase characters
- Return the number of characters in a string
- Locate a particular substring within a given string
- Return a Unicode character or code (page 241)
- Replace occurrences of a string with another string
- Reverse the order of a string
- Repeat a string a specified number of times

Performing Datetime and Interval Arithmetic

DBMS DBMS compliance with standard SQL datetime and interval operators and functions is spotty because DBMSs usually provide their own extended (nonstandard) operators and functions that perform date and time arithmetic.

Use the arithmetic operators (page 66) to perform datetime and interval arithmetic. The common temporal operations are:

- Subtracting two dates to calculate the interval between them
- Adding or subtracting an interval and a date to calculate a future or past date
- Adding or subtracting two intervals to get a new interval
- Multiplying or dividing an interval by a number to get a new interval

Some operations are undefined; adding two dates makes no sense, for example. Table 11.1 lists the valid SQL operators involving datetimes and intervals.

The standard SQL function EXTRACT() isolates a single field of a datetime or interval and returns it as a number. EXTRACT() typically is used in comparison expressions or for formatting results.

Table 11.1 Datetime and Interval Operations

Operation	Result
Datetime – Datetime	Interval
Datetime + Interval	Datetime
Datetime – Interval	Datetime
Interval + Datetime	Datetime
Interval + Interval	Interval
Interval – Interval	Interval
Interval * Numeric	Interval
Interval / Numeric	Interval
Numeric * Interval	Interval

To extract part of a datetime or interval, type:

```
EXTRACT(field FROM datetime_or_interval)
```

field is the part of *datetime_or_interval* to return. *field* is YEAR, MONTH, DAY, HOUR, MINUTE, SECOND, TIMEZONE_HOUR, or TIMEZONE_MINUTE. *datetime_or_interval* is a datetime or interval expression such as a column that contains datetime or interval values, a datetime or interval literal, or the result of an operation or function that returns a datetime or interval. If *field* is SECOND, EXTRACT() returns a NUMERIC value; otherwise, it returns an INTEGER. If any operand or argument is null, an expression returns null.

To list the books published in the first half of the years 2001 and 2002, sorted by descending publication date, type:

```
SELECT
    title_id,
    pubdate
  FROM titles
  WHERE EXTRACT(YEAR FROM pubdate)
        BETWEEN 2001 AND 2002
    AND EXTRACT(MONTH FROM pubdate)
        BETWEEN 1 AND 6
  ORDER BY pubdate DESC;
```

The result is:

```
title_id pubdate
-------- ----------
T09      2002-05-31
T08      2001-06-01
T05      2001-01-01
```

DBMS In **Microsoft Access** and **Microsoft SQL Server**, the extraction function is DATEPART(*datepart*, *date*). To run the preceding query, change the extraction expressions to `DATEPART("yyyy", pubdate)` and `DATEPART("m", pubdate)`.

Oracle, **MySQL**, and **PostgreSQL** accept different or additional values for the *field* argument of EXTRACT().

Instead of EXTRACT(), **DB2** extracts parts by using individual functions such as DAY(), HOUR(), and SECOND(). To run the preceding query, change the extraction expressions to `YEAR(pubdate)` and `MONTH(pubdate)`.

In addition to (or instead of) the standard arithmetic operators, DBMSs provide functions that add intervals to dates. Some examples: DATEDIFF() in **Microsoft Access** and **Microsoft SQL Server**, ADD_MONTHS() in **Oracle**, and DATE_ADD() and DATE_SUB() in **MySQL**.

Complex date and time arithmetic is so common in SQL programming that all DBMSs provide lots of temporal extensions. Search your DBMS documentation for *date and time functions* or *datetime functions*. Table 11.2 lists DBMS functions that return current date and time from the system clock of the particular computer where the DBMS is running.

Table 11.2 Getting the Current Date and Time

DBMS	Functions
Standard SQL	`CURRENT_DATE`, `CURRENT_TIME`, `CURRENT_TIMESTAMP`
Access	`Date()`, `Time()`, `Now()`
SQL Server	`CURRENT_TIMESTAMP` or `GETDATE()`
Oracle	`SYSDATE`, `CURRENT_DATE`, `CURRENT_TIMESTAMP`
DB2	`CURRENT_DATE`, `CURRENT_TIME`, `CURRENT_TIMESTAMP`
MySQL	`CURRENT_DATE`, `CURRENT_TIME`, `CURRENT_TIMESTAMP`
PostgreSQL	`CURRENT_DATE`, `CURRENT_TIME`, `CURRENT_TIMESTAMP`

Converting Data Types

In many situations, your DBMS will convert, or **cast**, data types automatically. It may allow you to use numbers and dates in character expressions such as concatenation, for example, or it will promote numbers automatically in mixed arithmetic expressions (see "Tips for arithmetic operations" on page 67). Use the function CAST() to convert an expression of one data type to another data type when your DBMS doesn't perform the conversion automatically. For information about data types, see Appendix C.

- **Implicit conversions** (or **coercions**) are those conversions that occur without specifying CAST(). **Explicit conversions** are those conversions that require CAST() to be specified. In some cases, conversion isn't allowed; you can't convert a FLOAT to a TIMESTAMP, for example.
- The data type being converted is the **source data type**, and the result data type is the **target data type**.
- You can convert any numeric or datetime data type to any character data type.
- You can convert any character data type to any other data type if the character string represents a valid literal value of the target data type. (DBMSs remove leading and trailing spaces when converting strings to numeric or datetime values.)
- Some numeric conversions, such as DECIMAL-to-INTEGER, round or truncate values. (Whether the value is rounded or truncated depends on the DBMS.)
- A VARCHAR-to-CHAR conversion can truncate strings.
- Some conversions can cause an error if the new data type doesn't have enough room to display the converted value. A FLOAT-to-SMALLINT conversion will fail if the floating-point number falls outside the range your DBMS allows for SMALLINT values.
- A NUMERIC-to-DECIMAL conversion can require an explicit cast to prevent the loss of precision or scale that might occur in an implicit conversion.
- In a DATE-to-TIMESTAMP conversion, the time part of the result will be 00:00:00 (midnight).
- If any argument is null, CAST() returns null. (But see the **Oracle** exception below.)

To convert one data type to another, type the function:

```
CAST(expr AS data_type)
```

expr is the expression to convert, and *data_type* is the target data type. *data_type* is one of the data types described in Appendix C and can include length, precision, or scale arguments where applicable. Acceptable *data_type* values include CHAR(10), VARCHAR(25), NUMERIC(5,2), INTEGER, FLOAT, and DATE, for example. An error occurs if the data type or value of *expr* is incompatible with *data_type*.

The following query converts the book prices from the DECIMAL data type to INTEGER and CHAR(8) data types. The < and > characters show the extent of the CHAR(8) strings. Your result will be either Result 1 or Result 2 depending on whether your DBMS truncates or rounds integers.

```
SELECT
    price
      AS "price(DECIMAL)",
    CAST(price AS INTEGER)
      AS "price(INTEGER)",
    '<' || CAST(price AS CHAR(8)) || '>'
      AS "price(CHAR(8))"
  FROM titles;
```

Result 1 (shortened for brevity)—you'll get this result if your DBMS *truncates* decimal numbers to convert them to integers:

```
price(DECIMAL) price(INTEGER) price(CHAR(8))
-------------- -------------- --------------
         21.99             21 <21.99    >
         19.95             19 <19.95    >
         39.95             39 <39.95    >
         12.99             12 <12.99    >
...
```

Result 2 (shortened for brevity)—you'll get this result if your DBMS *rounds* decimal numbers to convert them to integers:

```
price(DECIMAL) price(INTEGER) price(CHAR(8))
-------------- -------------- --------------
         21.99             22 <21.99    >
         19.95             20 <19.95    >
         39.95             40 <39.95    >
         12.99             13 <12.99    >
...
```

The following query lists history and biography book sales with a portion of the book title, sorted by descending sales (the CHAR(20) conversion shortens the title to make the result more readable):

```
SELECT
    CAST(sales AS CHAR(8))
    || ' copies sold of '
    || CAST(title_name AS CHAR(20))
      AS "History and biography sales"
  FROM titles
  WHERE sales IS NOT NULL
    AND type IN ('history', 'biography')
  ORDER BY sales DESC;
```

The result (shortened for brevity) is:

```
History and biography sales
--------------------------------------------
1500200  copies sold of I Blame My Mother
100001   copies sold of Spontaneous, Not Ann
11320    copies sold of How About Never?
...
```

DBMS **Microsoft Access** has a family of type-conversion functions rather than a single CAST() function: CStr(*expr*), CInt(*expr*), and CDec(*expr*) convert *expr* to a string, integer, and decimal number, for example. Use Space(*number*) to add spaces, Left(*string*, *length*) to truncate strings, and + to concatenate strings. Change the cast expressions to:

```
CInt(price)
```

```
'<' + CStr(price) + '>'
```

```
CStr(sales) + Space(8 - Len(CStr(sales))) +
' copies sold of ' + Left(title_name, 20)
```

Widening and Narrowing Conversions

Widening conversions are those conversions in which there is no possibility of data loss or incorrect results. SMALLINT-to-INTEGER, for example, is a widening conversion because the INTEGER data type can accommodate every possible value of the SMALLINT data type. The reverse operation, called a **narrowing conversion**, can cause data loss because extreme INTEGER values can't be represented by a SMALLINT. Widening conversions are always allowed, but narrowing conversions can cause your DBMS to issue a warning or error.

In **Microsoft SQL Server**, use + to concatenate strings:

```
'<' + CAST(price AS CHAR(8)) + '>'
```

```
CAST(sales AS CHAR(8)) + ' copies sold of ' +
CAST(title_name AS CHAR(20))
```

Oracle doesn't allow character conversions to CHAR(*length*) if *length* is shorter than the source string. Instead, use SUBSTR() to truncate strings. To run the preceding query, change the CAST() expression to:

```
CAST(sales AS CHAR(8)) || ' copies sold of ' ||
SUBSTR(title_name, 1, 20)
```

In **MySQL**, use SIGNED instead of INTEGER for *data_type*, and use CONCAT() to concatenate strings. Change the CAST() expressions to:

```
CAST(price AS SIGNED)
```

```
CONCAT('<', CAST(price AS CHAR(8)), '>')
```

```
CONCAT(CAST(sales AS CHAR(8)), ' copies sold of ',
CAST(title_name AS CHAR(20)))
```

For cast operations, **Oracle** treats an empty string as a null: CAST('' AS CHAR) returns NULL (not ''). See the DBMS tip in "Tips for nulls" on page 23.

In older **PostgreSQL** versions, to compare a value in a NUMERIC or DECIMAL column with a real (floating-point) number, you must convert the real number to NUMERIC or DECIMAL explicitly. The following statement, for example, fails in older PostgreSQL versions, because the data type of the column *price* is DECIMAL(5,2):

```
SELECT price
  FROM titles
  WHERE price < 20.00;
```

This statement fixes the problem:

```
SELECT price
  FROM titles
  WHERE price < CAST(20.00 AS DECIMAL);
```

DBMSs have additional conversion and formatting functions. Some examples: CONVERT() in **Microsoft SQL Server** and **MySQL**; TO_CHAR(), TO_DATE(), TO_TIMESTAMP(), and TO_NUMBER() in **Oracle** and **PostgreSQL**; and TO_CHAR() and TO_DATE() in **DB2**. Search your DBMS documentation for *conversion*, *cast*, or *formatting functions*.

CHAPTER 12

Evaluating Conditional Values

CASE Expressions

The CASE expression lets you take actions based on a condition's truth value (true, false, or unknown).

- If you've programmed before, you'll recognize that CASE provides SQL the equivalent of the *if-then-else*, *case*, or *switch* statements used in procedural languages, except that CASE is an expression, not a statement.
- CASE evaluates several conditions and returns a single value for the first true condition.
- CASE lets you display an alternative value to the actual value in a column. CASE makes no changes to the underlying data.
- A common use of CASE is to replace codes or abbreviations with more-readable values. If the column *marital_status* contains the integer codes 1, 2, 3, or 4—meaning single, married, divorced, or widowed—your human readers will prefer to see explanatory text rather than cryptic codes. (Some database designers prefer to use codes, because it's more efficient to store and manage abbreviated codes than explanatory text.)
- CASE has two formats: simple and searched. The **simple CASE** expression compares an expression to a set of simple expressions to determine the result. The **searched CASE** expression evaluates a set of logical (Boolean) expressions to determine the result.
- CASE returns an optional ELSE result as the default value if no test condition is true.

To use a simple CASE expression, type:

```
CASE comparison_value
  WHEN value1 THEN result1
  WHEN value2 THEN result2
  ...
  WHEN valueN THEN resultN
  [ELSE default_result]
END
```

value1, value2,..., valueN are expressions. *result1, result2,..., resultN* are expressions returned when the corresponding value matches the expression *comparison_value*. All expressions must be of the same type or must be implicitly convertible to the same type.

Each value is compared to *comparison_value* in order. First, *value1* is compared. If it matches *comparison_value*, then *result1* is returned; otherwise, *value2* is compared to *comparison_value*. If *value2* matches *comparison_value*, then *result2* is returned, and so on. If no matches occur, *default_result* is returned. If ELSE *default_result* is omitted, ELSE NULL is assumed.

To raise the price of history books by 10 percent and psychology books by 20 percent, and leave the prices of other books unchanged, type:

```
SELECT title_id, type, price,
    CASE type
      WHEN 'history'    THEN price * 1.10
      WHEN 'psychology' THEN price * 1.20
      ELSE price
    END
      AS "New price"
  FROM titles
  ORDER BY type ASC, title_id ASC;
```

The result (shortened for brevity) is:

```
title_id type       price New price
-------- ---------- ----- ---------
...
T09      children   13.95     13.95
T03      computer   39.95     39.95
T01      history    21.99     24.19
T02      history    19.95     21.95
T13      history    29.99     32.99
T04      psychology 12.99     15.59
...
```

To use a searched CASE expression, type:

```
CASE
  WHEN condition1 THEN result1
  WHEN condition2 THEN result2
  ...
  WHEN conditionN THEN resultN
  [ELSE default_result]
END
```

condition1, *condition2*,..., *conditionN* are search conditions (Chapter 6). *result1*, *result2*,..., *resultN* are expressions returned when the corresponding condition evaluates to true. All expressions must be of the same type or must be implicitly convertible to the same type.

Each condition is evaluated in order. First, *condition1* is evaluated. If it's true, *result1* is returned; otherwise, *condition2* is evaluated. If *condition2* is true, *result2* is returned, and so on. If no conditions are true, *default_result* is returned. If ELSE *default_result* is omitted, ELSE NULL is assumed.

To list the books categorized by different sales ranges, sorted by ascending sales, type:

```
SELECT title_id,
    CASE
      WHEN sales IS NULL   THEN 'Unknown'
      WHEN sales <= 1000   THEN 'Not more than 1,000'
      WHEN sales <= 10000  THEN 'Between 1,001 and 10,000'
      WHEN sales <= 100000 THEN 'Between 10,001 and 100,000'
      WHEN sales <= 1000000
        THEN 'Between 100,001 and 1,000,000'
      ELSE 'Over 1,000,000'
    END
      AS "Sales category"
  FROM titles
  ORDER BY sales ASC;
```

The result (shortened for brevity) is:

```
title_id Sales category
-------- -----------------------------
T10      Unknown
T01      Not more than 1,000
T08      Between 1,001 and 10,000
T09      Between 1,001 and 10,000
...
```

Tips for CASE

- When a result is returned, CASE may or may not evaluate the expressions in any remaining WHEN clauses, depending on the DBMS. For this reason, you should watch for undesirable side effects, such as the evaluation of any expression resulting in a division-by-zero error.
- This CASE expression can help you prevent division-by-zero errors:

```
CASE
  WHEN n <> 0 THEN expr/n
  ELSE NULL
END
```

- The simple CASE expression is just shorthand for this searched CASE expression:

```
CASE
  WHEN comparison_value = value1 THEN result1
  WHEN comparison_value = value2 THEN result2
  ...
  WHEN comparison_value = valueN THEN resultN
  [ELSE default_result]
END
```

- **DBMS** **Microsoft Access** doesn't support CASE; instead, use the function Switch(*condition1*, *result1*, *condition2*, *result2*,...). For example, to run the first example query, change the CASE expression to:

```
Switch(
type IS NULL, NULL,
type = 'history', price * 1.10,
type = 'psychology', price * 1.20,
type IN ('biography', 'children', 'computer'), price)
```

Oracle 9i and later will run the example queries. To run the first example query in Oracle 8i and earlier, translate the simple CASE expression to a searched CASE expression, or use the function DECODE(*comparison_value*, *value1*, *result1*, *value2*, *result2*,..., *default_result*):

```
DECODE(type,
NULL, NULL,
'history', price * 1.10,
'psychology', price * 1.20,
price)
```

CHAPTER 13

Summarizing Data

Understanding Aggregate Functions

The preceding chapters used **scalar functions**, which operate on individual row values. This chapter introduces SQL's **aggregate functions**, or **set functions**, which operate on a group of values to produce a single, summarizing value. You apply an aggregate to a set of rows, which can be:

- All the rows in a table
- Only those rows specified by a WHERE clause
- Those rows created by a GROUP BY clause (Chapter 14)

The main difference between queries with and without aggregate functions is that nonaggregate queries process the rows one by one. Each row is processed independently and put into the result. (ORDER BY and DISTINCT make the DBMS look at all the rows, but they're essentially postprocessing operations.) Aggregate queries do something completely different: they take a table as a whole and construct new rows from it.

Table 13.1 lists SQL's standard aggregate functions.

- In Table 13.1, the expression *expr* often is a column name, but it also can be a literal, function, or any combination of chained or nested column names, literals, and functions.
- SUM() and AVG() work with only numeric data types. MIN() and MAX() work with character, numeric, and datetime data types. COUNT(*expr*) and COUNT(*) work with all data types.
- All aggregate functions except COUNT(*) ignore nulls (page 22).
- COUNT(*expr*) and COUNT(*) never return null but return either a positive integer or zero. The other aggregate functions return null if the set contains no rows or contains rows with only nulls.
- Default column headings for aggregate expressions vary by DBMS; use AS (page 28) to name the result column.
- **DBMS** DBMSs provide additional aggregate functions to calculate other statistics, such as the standard deviation; search your DBMS documentation for *aggregate functions* or *group functions*.

Aggregate functions can be tricky to use. The following examples explain what's legal and what's not.

- An aggregate expression *can't* appear in a WHERE clause. If you want to find the title of the book with the highest sales, you *can't* use:

```
SELECT title_id                    --Illegal
  FROM titles
  WHERE sales = MAX(sales);
```

Table 13.1 Aggregate Functions

Function	Returns
MIN(*expr*)	Minimum value in *expr*
MAX(*expr*)	Maximum value in *expr*
SUM(*expr*)	Sum of the values in *expr*
AVG(*expr*)	Average (arithmetic mean) of the values in *expr*
COUNT(*expr*)	The number of non-null values in *expr*
COUNT(*)	The number of rows in a table or set

- You *can't* mix nonaggregate (row-by-row) and aggregate expressions in a SELECT clause. A SELECT clause must contain either all nonaggregate expressions or all aggregate expressions. If you want to find the title of the book with the highest sales, you *can't* use:

```
SELECT title_id, MAX(sales)
  FROM titles;                        --Illegal
```

  The one exception to this rule is that you *can* mix nonaggregate and aggregate expressions for grouping columns (Chapter 14):

```
SELECT type, SUM(sales)
  FROM titles
  GROUP BY type;                        --Legal
```

- You *can* use more than one aggregate expression in a SELECT clause:

```
SELECT MIN(sales), MAX(sales)
  FROM titles;                          --Legal
```

- You *can't* nest aggregate functions:

```
SELECT SUM(AVG(sales))
  FROM titles;                        --Illegal
```

- You *can* use aggregate expressions in subqueries (Chapter 17). This statement finds the title of the book with the highest sales:

```
SELECT title_id, price                --Legal
  FROM titles
  WHERE sales = (SELECT MAX(sales) FROM titles);
```

- You *can't* use subqueries in aggregate expressions:

```
AVG(SELECT price FROM titles)  --Illegal
```

- **DBMS** **Oracle** lets you nest aggregate expressions in GROUP BY queries (Chapter 14). The following example calculates the average of the maximum sales of all book types:

```
SELECT AVG(MAX(sales))
  FROM titles
  GROUP BY type;          --Legal in Oracle
```

  To replicate this query in standard SQL, use a subquery:

```
SELECT AVG(s.max_sales)
  FROM (SELECT MAX(sales) AS max_sales
          FROM titles
          GROUP BY type) s;
```

Using Aggregate Functions

To list the price of the lowest-priced book, type:

```
SELECT MIN(price) AS "Min price"
  FROM titles;
```

The result is:

```
Min price
---------
     6.95
```

To list the highest revenue (= price × sales) among the history books, type:

```
SELECT MAX(price * sales) AS "Max history revenue"
  FROM titles
  WHERE type = 'history';
```

The result is:

```
Max history revenue
-------------------
          313905.33
```

To list the total price, sales, and revenue (= price × sales) of all books, type:

```
SELECT
    SUM(price) AS "Total price",
    SUM(sales) AS "Total sales",
    SUM(price * sales) AS "Total revenue"
  FROM titles;
```

The result is:

```
Total price Total sales Total revenue
----------- ----------- -------------
     220.65     1975446   41428860.77
```

Note a mathematical rule in action in the preceding result: "The sum of the products doesn't (necessarily) equal the product of the sums."

To use a subquery (Chapter 17) to list the books with above-average sales, type:

```
SELECT title_id, sales
  FROM titles
  WHERE sales > (SELECT AVG(sales) FROM titles)
  ORDER BY sales DESC;
```

The result is:

```
title_id sales
-------- -------
T07      1500200
T05       201440
```

Tip: The sum and average of no rows is null—not zero, as you might expect.

The following three queries count rows in the table *titles* and are identical except for the WHERE clause:

```
SELECT
    COUNT(title_id) AS "COUNT(title_id)",
    COUNT(price) AS "COUNT(price)",
    COUNT(*) AS "COUNT(*)"
  FROM titles;

SELECT
    COUNT(title_id) AS "COUNT(title_id)",
    COUNT(price) AS "COUNT(price)",
    COUNT(*) AS "COUNT(*)"
  FROM titles
  WHERE price IS NOT NULL;

SELECT
    COUNT(title_id) AS "COUNT(title_id)",
    COUNT(price) AS "COUNT(price)",
    COUNT(*) AS "COUNT(*)"
  FROM titles
  WHERE price IS NULL;
```

The row counts in the results vary because the column *price* contains a null (page 22):

```
COUNT(title_id) COUNT(price) COUNT(*)
--------------- ------------ --------
             13           12       13

COUNT(title_id) COUNT(price) COUNT(*)
--------------- ------------ --------
             12           12       12

COUNT(title_id) COUNT(price) COUNT(*)
--------------- ------------ --------
              1            0        1
```

Aggregating Distinct Values

You can use DISTINCT (page 29) to eliminate duplicate values in aggregate function calculations. The general syntax of an aggregate function is:

agg_func([ALL | DISTINCT] *expr*)

agg_func is MIN, MAX, SUM, AVG, or COUNT. *expr* is a column name, literal, or expression. ALL applies the aggregate function to all values, and DISTINCT specifies that each unique value is considered. ALL is the default and is usually omitted in practice.

With SUM(), AVG(), and COUNT(*expr*), DISTINCT eliminates duplicate values before the sum, average, or count is calculated. DISTINCT isn't meaningful with MIN() and MAX(); you can use it, but it won't change the result. You can't use DISTINCT with COUNT(*).

The following queries return the count, sum, and average of book prices:

```
SELECT COUNT(*) AS "COUNT(*)"
  FROM titles;

SELECT
    COUNT(price) AS "COUNT(price)",
    SUM(price)   AS "SUM(price)",
    AVG(price)   AS "AVG(price)"
  FROM titles;

SELECT
    COUNT(DISTINCT price) AS "COUNT(DISTINCT)",
    SUM(DISTINCT price)   AS "SUM(DISTINCT)",
    AVG(DISTINCT price)   AS "AVG(DISTINCT)"
  FROM titles;
```

The non-DISTINCT and DISTINCT results differ because the DISTINCT results eliminate the duplicates of prices $12.99 and $19.95 from calculations (note that the column *price* contains a null (page 22)):

```
COUNT(*)
--------
      13

COUNT(price) SUM(price) AVG(price)
------------ ---------- ----------
          12     220.65    18.3875

COUNT(DISTINCT) SUM(DISTINCT) AVG(DISTINCT)
--------------- ------------- -------------
             10        187.71       18.7710
```

CHAPTER 14

Grouping Data

Grouping Rows with GROUP BY

In Chapter 13, aggregate functions were used to summarize all the values in a column or just those values that matched a WHERE search condition. You can also use the GROUP BY clause to divide a table into logical **groups** (categories) and calculate aggregate statistics for each group.

The following query, for example, uses GROUP BY to count the number of books that each author wrote (or cowrote). In the SELECT clause, the column *au_id* identifies each author, and the derived column *num_books* counts each author's books. The GROUP BY clause causes *num_books* to be calculated for every unique *au_id* instead of only once for the entire table.

```
SELECT
    au_id,
    COUNT(*) AS "num_books"
  FROM title_authors
  GROUP BY au_id;
```

In the result, *au_id* is called the **grouping column**:

```
au_id num_books
----- ---------
A01           3
A02           4
A03           2
A04           4
A05           1
A06           3
```

In a SELECT statement (page 25), the GROUP BY clause comes after the WHERE clause and before the ORDER BY clause.

- Grouping columns can be column names or derived columns.
- No columns from the input table can appear in an aggregate query's SELECT clause unless they're also included in the GROUP BY clause. A column has (or can have) different values in different rows, so there's no way to decide which of these values to include in the result if you're generating a single new row from the table as a whole. The following statement is illegal because GROUP BY returns only one row for each value of *type*; the query can't return the multiple values of *pub_id* that are associated with each value of *type*:

```
SELECT type, pub_id, COUNT(*)
  FROM titles
  GROUP BY type;              --Illegal
```

- If the SELECT clause contains a complex nonaggregate expression (more than just a simple column name), the GROUP BY expression must match the SELECT expression exactly.
- To nest groups, specify multiple, comma-separated grouping columns in the GROUP BY clause. Data are summarized at the final specified group.
- If a grouping column contains a null (page 22), that row becomes a group in the result. If a grouping column contains more than one null, the nulls are put into a single group. A group that contains multiple nulls doesn't imply that the nulls equal one another.
- To eliminate rows before grouping occurs, use a WHERE clause in a query containing a GROUP BY clause.
- You can't use a column alias (page 28) in the GROUP BY clause, though table aliases (page 99) are allowed as qualifiers.
- Without an ORDER BY clause (Chapter 5), groups returned by GROUP BY aren't in any particular order. To sort the result of the preceding query by the descending number of books, for example, add the clause `ORDER BY "num_books" DESC`.

Using GROUP BY

The following query shows the difference between COUNT(*expr*) and COUNT(*) in a query that contains GROUP BY. The table *publishers* contains one null in the column *state* (for publisher P03 in Germany). Recall from

Chapter 13 that COUNT(*expr*) counts non-null values and COUNT(*) counts all values, including nulls. In the result, GROUP BY recognizes the null and creates a null group for it. COUNT(*) finds (and counts) the one null in the column *state*. But COUNT(state) contains a zero for the null group because COUNT(state) finds only a null in the null group, which it excludes from the count—that's why you have the zero.

```
SELECT
    state,
    COUNT(state) AS "COUNT(state)",
    COUNT(*)     AS "COUNT(*)"
  FROM publishers
  GROUP BY state;
```

The result is:

```
state COUNT(state) COUNT(*)
----- ------------ --------
NULL             0        1
CA               2        2
NY               1        1
```

The following query calculates the total sales, average sales, and number of titles for each type of book. The WHERE clause eliminates books priced less than $13 before grouping. The ORDER BY clause sorts the result by descending total sales of each book type.

```
SELECT
    type,
    SUM(sales)   AS "SUM(sales)",
    AVG(sales)   AS "AVG(sales)",
    COUNT(sales) AS "COUNT(sales)"
  FROM titles
  WHERE price >= 13
  GROUP BY type
  ORDER BY "SUM(sales)" DESC;
```

The result is:

```
type       SUM(sales) AVG(sales) COUNT(sales)
---------- ---------- ---------- ------------
biography     1511520  755760.00            2
computer        25667   25667.00            1
history         20599    6866.33            3
children         5000    5000.00            1
```

The following query uses multiple grouping columns to count the number of titles of each type that each publisher publishes.

```
SELECT pub_id, type, COUNT(*) AS "COUNT(*)"
  FROM titles
  GROUP BY pub_id, type
  ORDER BY pub_id ASC, "COUNT(*)" DESC;
```

The result is:

```
pub_id type       COUNT(*)
------ ---------- --------
P01    biography         3
P01    history           1
P02    computer          1
P03    history           2
P03    biography         1
P04    psychology        3
P04    children          2
```

Filtering Groups with HAVING

The HAVING clause sets conditions on the GROUP BY clause similar to the way that WHERE interacts with SELECT.

- In a SELECT statement (page 25), the HAVING clause comes after the GROUP BY clause and before the ORDER BY clause.
- Just as WHERE limits the number of rows displayed by SELECT, HAVING limits the number of groups displayed by GROUP BY.
- The WHERE search condition is applied *before* grouping occurs, and the HAVING search condition is applied *after*.
- HAVING syntax is similar to the WHERE syntax, except that HAVING can contain aggregate functions.
- A HAVING clause can reference any of the items that appear in the SELECT list.

The sequence in which the WHERE, GROUP BY, and HAVING clauses are applied is:

1. The WHERE clause filters the rows that result from the operations specified in the FROM and JOIN clauses.
2. The GROUP BY clause groups the output of the WHERE clause.
3. The HAVING clause filters rows from the grouped result.

To filter groups, use a HAVING clause of the form:

HAVING *search_condition*

search_condition is a search condition used to filter groups. *search_condition* can contain aggregate functions (Chapter 13) but otherwise is identical to the WHERE search condition (Chapter 6 and subsequent chapters). You can combine and negate multiple HAVING conditions with the logical operators AND, OR, and NOT (Chapter 7).

The HAVING search condition is applied to the rows in the output produced by grouping. Only the groups that meet the search condition appear in the result. You can apply a HAVING clause only to columns that appear in the GROUP BY clause or in an aggregate function.

Using HAVING

To list the number of books written (or cowritten) by each author who has written three or more books, type:

```
SELECT
    au_id,
    COUNT(*) AS "num_books"
  FROM title_authors
  GROUP BY au_id
  HAVING COUNT(*) >= 3;
```

The result is:

```
au_id num_books
----- ---------
A01           3
A02           4
A04           4
A06           3
```

To list the number of titles and average revenue for the types with average revenue more than $1 million, type:

```
SELECT
    type,
    COUNT(price) AS "COUNT(price)",
    AVG(price * sales) AS "AVG revenue"
  FROM titles
  GROUP BY type
  HAVING AVG(price * sales) > 1000000;
```

The result is:

```
type       COUNT(price) AVG revenue
---------- ------------ -----------
biography             3 12484878.00
computer              1  1025396.65
```

To list the number of books of each type for each publisher, for publishers with more than one title of a type, type:

```
SELECT
    pub_id,
    type,
    COUNT(*) AS "COUNT(*)"
  FROM titles
  GROUP BY pub_id, type
  HAVING COUNT(*) > 1
  ORDER BY pub_id ASC, "COUNT(*)" DESC;
```

The result is:

```
pub_id type       COUNT(*)
------ ---------- --------
P01    biography         3
P03    history           2
P04    psychology        3
P04    children          2
```

For books from only publishers P03 and P04, the following query lists the total sales and average price by type, for types with more than $10000 total sales and less than $20 average price.

```
SELECT
    type,
    SUM(sales) AS "SUM(sales)",
    AVG(price) AS "AVG(price)"
  FROM titles
  WHERE pub_id IN ('P03', 'P04')
  GROUP BY type
  HAVING SUM(sales) > 10000
     AND AVG(price) < 20;
```

The result is:

```
type       SUM(sales) AVG(price)
---------- ---------- ----------
psychology     308564       9.31
```

CHAPTER 15

Joining Tables

Understanding Joins

All the queries so far have retrieved rows from a single table. This chapter explains how to use joins to retrieve rows from multiple tables simultaneously. Recall from Chapter 2 that information about different entities (authors, movies, invoices, appointments, and so on) is stored in different tables. A **relationship** is an association established between common columns in two tables. A **join** is a table operation that uses related columns to combine rows from two input tables into one result table. You can chain joins to retrieve rows from an unlimited number of tables.

Why do joins matter? The most important database information isn't so much stored in the rows of individual tables; rather, it's the implied relationships between sets of related rows. In the sample database, for example, the individual rows of the tables *authors*, *publishers*, and *titles* contain important values, of course, but it's the implied relationships that let you understand and analyze your data in its entirety: Who wrote what? Who published what? To whom do we send royalty checks? For how much? And so on. This chapter explains the different types of joins, why they're used, and how to create a SELECT statement that uses them.

Tip: It's possible to consolidate all information about any entity type into a single monolithic table, but that table would be loaded with duplicate data. Redundancy is the enemy of database users and administrators: it causes databases to grow wildly large, it slows queries, and it's a maintenance and reporting nightmare. (When someone moves, you want to change her address in one place, not thousands of places.)

Qualifying Column Names

Recall from "Columns" on page 10 that column names must be unique within a table but can be reused in other tables. The tables *authors* and *publishers* in the sample database both contain a column named *city*, for example.

To identify an otherwise-ambiguous column uniquely in a query that involves multiple tables, use its qualified name. A **qualified name** is a table name followed by a dot and the name of the column in the table:

```
table.column
```

Because tables must have different names within a database, a qualified name identifies a single column uniquely within the entire database.

The qualified names in the following query resolve otherwise-ambiguous references to the column *city* in the tables *authors* and *publishers*:

```
SELECT au_id, authors.city
  FROM authors
  INNER JOIN publishers
    ON authors.city = publishers.city;
```

The result lists authors who live in the same city as some publisher (the join syntax is explained later in this chapter):

```
au_id city
----- -------------
A03   San Francisco
A04   San Francisco
A05   New York
```

Tip: You can mix qualified and unqualified names within the same statement.

Qualified names aren't required if there's no chance of ambiguity—that is, if the query's tables have no column names in common. To improve system performance, however, qualify *all* columns in a query with joins.

Creating Table Aliases with AS

You can create table aliases by using AS just as you can create column aliases (page 28). Table aliases:

- Save typing
- Reduce statement clutter
- Exist only for the duration of a statement
- Don't appear in the result (unlike column aliases)
- Don't change the name of a table in the database
- Also are called **correlation names** in the context of subqueries (Chapter 17)

To create a table alias, in a FROM clause or JOIN clause, type:

```
table [AS] alias
```

table is a table name, and *alias* is its alias name. *alias* is a single, unquoted word that contains only letters, digits, or underscores; don't use spaces, punctuation, or special characters. The AS keyword is optional.

DBMS In **Oracle**, you must omit the keyword AS when you create a table alias. For DBMS portability, all the examples in this book omit the keyword AS.

The table aliases in the following query are short and easy to read. Note that you can use an alias in the SELECT clause before it's actually defined later in the statement.

```
SELECT au_fname, au_lname, a.city
  FROM authors a
  INNER JOIN publishers p
    ON a.city = p.city;
```

Each table's alias must be unique within the same SQL statement. In practice, table aliases are short (typically, one or two characters), but long names are valid.

An alias name hides a table name. If you alias a table, you must use its alias in all qualified references. The following statement is illegal because the alias *a* occludes the table name *authors*:

```
SELECT authors.au_id
  FROM authors a;           --Illegal
```

Using Joins

You can use a join to extract data from more than one table. This chapter and the next one explain the different types of joins (Table 15.1), why they're used, and how to create SELECT statements that use them.

- The two join **operands** (input tables) usually are called the first table and the second table, but they are called the left table and the right table in outer joins, in which table order matters.
- Tables are joined row by row and side by side by satisfying whatever join condition(s) you specify in the query. Rows that don't match are included or excluded, depending on the type of join.
- A **theta join** uses a comparison operator (=, <>, <, <=, >, or >=) to compare values in joined columns. An **equijoin**, the most common type of join, is a theta join that compares values for equality.
- A join's connecting columns often are associated key columns, but you can join any columns with compatible data types (except for cross joins, which require no specific join columns). Joined columns needn't have the same column name.
- To ensure that a join is meaningful, compare values in columns defined over the same domain (page 10). It's possible to join the columns *titles.price* and *royalties.advance*, for example, but the result will be meaningless. A typical join condition specifies a foreign key in one table and the associated primary key in the other table (page 13). If a key is composite (has multiple columns), you can (and normally should) join all the key's columns.
- You can nest and chain joins to join more than two tables, but understand that the DBMS works its way through your query by executing joins on exactly two tables at a time. The two tables in each join can be two base tables from the database, a base table and a table that is the result of a previous join, or two tables that are the results of previous joins.
- The SQL standard doesn't limit the number of tables (or joins) that can appear in a query, but your DBMS will have built-in limits, or your database administrator might set limits that are lower than the built-in limits.
- If a join's connecting columns contain nulls (page 22), the nulls never join. Nulls represent unknown values that aren't considered to be equal (or unequal) to one another. Nulls in a column from one of the joined tables can be returned only by using a cross join or an outer join (unless a WHERE clause excludes null values explicitly).

- Joins exist only for the duration of a query and aren't part of the database or DBMS.
- The data types (Appendix C) of the join columns must be compatible, meaning that the DBMS can convert values to a common type for comparisons. For most DBMSs, numeric data types (INTEGER, FLOAT, and NUMERIC, for example), character data types (CHAR, VARCHAR), and datetime data types (DATE, TIMESTAMP) are compatible. You can't join binary objects. Conversions require computational overhead. For the best performance, the join columns should have *identical* data types, including whether nulls are allowed.

Table 15.1 Types of Joins

Join	Description
Cross join	Returns all rows from the first table in which each row from the first table is combined with all rows from the second table.
Inner join	A join that uses a comparison operator to match rows from two tables based on the values in common columns from each table. Inner joins are the most common type of join.
Left outer join	Returns *all* the rows from the left table, not just the ones in which the joined columns match. If a row in the left table has no matching rows in the right table, the associated result row contains nulls for all SELECT-clause columns coming from the right table.
Right outer join	The reverse of a left outer join. All rows from the right table are returned. Nulls are returned for the left table if a right-table row has no matching left-table row.
Full outer join	Returns all rows in both the left and right tables. If a row has no match in the other table, the SELECT-clause columns from the other table contain nulls. If there is a match between the tables, the entire result row contains values from both tables.
Self-join	A join of a table to itself.

Creating Joins with JOIN or WHERE

You have two alternative ways of specifying a join: by using JOIN syntax or WHERE syntax. SQL-92 and later standards prescribe JOIN syntax, but older standards prescribe WHERE; hence, both JOIN and WHERE are used widely and are legal in most DBMSs.

This section explains the general syntax for JOIN and WHERE joins that involve two tables. The actual syntax that you'll use in real queries will vary by the join type, the number of columns joined, the number of tables joined, and the syntax requirements of your DBMS. The examples in the following chapter show you how to create specific joins.

To create a join by using JOIN, type:

```
SELECT columns
  FROM table1 join_type table2
    ON join_conditions
  [WHERE search_condition]
  [GROUP BY grouping_columns]
  [HAVING search_condition]
  [ORDER BY sort_columns];
```

columns is one or more comma-separated expressions or column names from *table1* or *table2*. If *table1* and *table2* have a column name in common, you must qualify all references to these columns throughout the query to prevent ambiguity (page 98).

table1 and *table2* are the names of the joined tables. You can alias the table names (page 99).

join_type specifies what kind of join is performed: CROSS JOIN, INNER JOIN, LEFT OUTER JOIN, RIGHT OUTER JOIN, or FULL OUTER JOIN.

join_conditions specifies one or more join conditions to be evaluated for each pair of joined rows. (The ON clause isn't allowed in cross joins.) A join condition takes this form:

```
[table1.]column op [table2.]column
```

op usually is = but can be any comparison operator: =, <>, <, <=, >, or >= (page 40). You can combine multiple join conditions with AND or OR (Chapter 7).

To create a join by using WHERE, type:

```
SELECT columns
  FROM table1, table2
  WHERE join_conditions
  [GROUP BY grouping_columns]
  [HAVING search_condition]
  [ORDER BY sort_columns];
```

columns, *table1*, and *table2* have the same meaning as in JOIN syntax.

join_conditions also has the same meaning as in JOIN syntax, except that *op* can be a special symbol that indicates the join type. The WHERE clause also can include (nonjoin) search conditions to filter rows (page 41).

The following two statements show equivalent queries that use JOIN and WHERE syntax.

```
-- A join that uses JOIN syntax
SELECT au_fname, au_lname, a.city
  FROM authors a
  INNER JOIN publishers p
    ON a.city = p.city;
```

```
-- The same join, using WHERE syntax
SELECT au_fname, au_lname, a.city
  FROM authors a, publishers p
  WHERE a.city = p.city;
```

The result (of either statement) lists the authors who live in the same city in which a publisher is located:

```
au_fname  au_lname city
--------- -------- -------------
Hallie    Hull     San Francisco
Klee      Hull     San Francisco
Christian Kells    New York
```

Tips for JOIN and WHERE

- It might seem odd to use a WHERE clause to specify join conditions, but the join condition *does* act as a filter. When you join two tables, the DBMS internally pairs every row in the left table with every row in the right table, forming a cross join (page 107). The DBMS then uses the join condition to filter rows from the cross join (conceptually, anyway; DBMS optimizers don't actually create enormous cross-joined tables for every join).
- The compelling reason to prefer JOIN to WHERE syntax is that JOIN makes the join type explicit. A LEFT OUTER JOIN B is clearer than, say, A *= B. For the most common type of joins—simple inner joins—I think that WHERE syntax is easier to understand, however. Both JOIN and WHERE syntax are popular, so you'll have to learn both to read queries created by other people.
- In a three-table join, only one table can be used to bridge from one of the other tables to the third table.
- The SELECT-clause list for a join can reference all the columns in the joined tables or any subset of the columns. The list isn't required to contain columns from every table in the join. In a three-table join, for example, none of the columns from the middle table needs to be in the list.

Query Execution Sequence

When your DBMS processes joins, it uses a logical sequence to execute the entire query.

The DBMS:

1. Applies the join conditions in the JOIN clause.
2. Applies the join conditions and search conditions in the WHERE clause.
3. Groups rows according to the GROUP BY clause.
4. Applies the search conditions in the HAVING clause to the groups.
5. Sorts the result according to the ORDER BY clause.

- Joined columns don't need to have the same data type (Appendix C). If the data types aren't identical, they must be compatible or must be data types that your DBMS can convert implicitly to a common type. If the data types can't be converted implicitly, the join condition must convert the data type explicitly by using the CAST() function (page 77).
- If you're using WHERE syntax with two or more join conditions, you'll almost always want to combine all the join conditions with AND. Combining join conditions with OR is legal, but the result is hard to interpret. For more information about AND and OR, see Chapter 7.
- Most queries that use joins can be rewritten by using a subquery (a query nested within another query), and most subqueries can be rewritten as joins. For information about subqueries, see Chapter 17.
- **DBMS** **Oracle** 8i and earlier don't support JOIN syntax; use WHERE joins instead. Oracle 9i and later support JOIN syntax.

  Your DBMS might prohibit joins on columns with particular data types (especially binary and long-text data types). **Microsoft SQL Server** prohibits joins on ntext, text, and image columns, and **Oracle** prohibits joins on LOB columns, for example. Search your DBMS documentation for *joins*.

Domains and Comparisons

The values that you compare in joins and WHERE clauses must be *meaningfully* comparable—that is, have the same data type *and* the same meaning. The sample-database columns *au_id* and *pub_id*, for example, have the same data type—both are CHAR(3), a letter followed by two digits—but mean different things, so they can't be compared sensibly.

Recall from "Columns" on page 10 that a domain is the set of permissible values for a column. To prevent meaningless comparisons, the relational model requires that comparable columns draw from domains that have the same meaning. Unfortunately, SQL and DBMSs stray from the model and have no intrinsic mechanism that prevents users from comparing, say, IQ and shoe size. If you're building a database application, it's up to you to stop (or warn) users from making meaningless comparisons that waste processing time or, worse, yield results that might be interpreted as valid.

CHAPTER 16

Working with Joins

Creating a Cross Join with CROSS JOIN

A **cross join** (also called a **Cartesian product** or **cross product**) returns all possible combinations of rows of two tables. The result contains all rows from the first table; *each* row from the first table is combined with *all* rows from the second table. Because cross joins don't use a join condition, you omit the ON clause if you're using JOIN syntax, or omit the WHERE clause if you're using WHERE syntax.

A cross join is seldom used alone because the result is cumbersome and hard to interpret but does appear in some types of queries as an intermediate result.

Tip: Cross joins can produce a huge result, even with small tables. If one table has *m* rows and the other has *n* rows, the result contains $m \times n$ rows. For large tables, cross joins are computationally expensive and time-consuming queries. If a result contains an unexpectedly large number of rows, you might have omitted a join condition from your query accidentally and produced a cross product.

The following query uses a cross join to list all possible combinations of rows from the tables *authors* and *publishers*:

```
SELECT au_id, pub_id,
    a.state AS "au_state", p.state AS "pub_state"
  FROM authors a
  CROSS JOIN publishers p;
```

Using WHERE syntax, the equivalent query is:

```
SELECT au_id, pub_id,
    a.state AS "au_state", p.state AS "pub_state"
  FROM authors a, publishers p;
```

The result (shortened for brevity) is:

```
au_id pub_id au_state pub_state
----- ------ -------- ---------
A01   P01    NY       NY
A02   P01    CO       NY
A03   P01    CA       NY
A04   P01    CA       NY
A05   P01    NY       NY
A06   P01    CA       NY
A07   P01    FL       NY
A01   P02    NY       CA
A02   P02    CO       CA
A03   P02    CA       CA
A04   P02    CA       CA
A05   P02    NY       CA
A06   P02    CA       CA
A07   P02    FL       CA
A01   P03    NY       NULL
A02   P03    CO       NULL
A03   P03    CA       NULL
A04   P03    CA       NULL
A05   P03    NY       NULL
A06   P03    CA       NULL
A07   P03    FL       NULL
A01   P04    NY       CA
...
```

To find the cross product of *n* tables by using JOIN syntax, type:

```
SELECT columns
  FROM table1
  CROSS JOIN table2
  ...
  CROSS JOIN tableN
```

Equivalently, using WHERE syntax:

```
SELECT columns
  FROM table1, table2,..., tableN
```

Creating an Inner Join with INNER JOIN

An **inner join** uses a comparison operator (=, <>, <, <=, >, or >=) to match rows from two tables based on the values in common columns from each table. You can retrieve all rows in which the author identifier (the column *au_id*) is the same in both the tables *authors* and *title_authors*, for example. The result contains only joined rows that satisfy the join condition(s).

The following query joins two tables on the column *au_id* to list the books that each author wrote (or cowrote). Each author's *au_id* in the table *authors* matches zero or more rows in the table *title_authors*. Note that author A07 (Paddy O'Furniture) is omitted from the result because he has written no books and so has no matching rows in *title_authors*.

```
SELECT a.au_id, a.au_fname, a.au_lname, ta.title_id
  FROM authors a
  INNER JOIN title_authors ta
    ON a.au_id = ta.au_id
  ORDER BY a.au_id ASC, ta.title_id ASC;
```

Using WHERE syntax, the equivalent query is:

```
SELECT a.au_id, a.au_fname, a.au_lname, ta.title_id
  FROM authors a, title_authors ta
  WHERE a.au_id = ta.au_id
  ORDER BY a.au_id ASC, ta.title_id ASC;
```

The result (shortened for brevity) is:

```
au_id au_fname  au_lname  title_id
----- --------- --------- --------
A01   Sarah     Buchman   T01
A01   Sarah     Buchman   T02
A01   Sarah     Buchman   T13
A02   Wendy     Heydemark T06
A02   Wendy     Heydemark T07
A02   Wendy     Heydemark T10
A02   Wendy     Heydemark T12
A03   Hallie    Hull      T04
A03   Hallie    Hull      T11
A04   Klee      Hull      T04
...
A05   Christian Kells     T03
A06             Kellsey   T08
A06             Kellsey   T09
A06             Kellsey   T11
```

The following query uses two join conditions to list the authors who live in the same city and state as some publisher (any publisher).

```
SELECT a.au_id, a.au_fname, a.au_lname, a.city, a.state
  FROM authors a
  INNER JOIN publishers p
    ON a.city = p.city
    AND a.state = p.state
  ORDER BY a.au_id;
```

Using WHERE syntax, the equivalent query is:

```
SELECT a.au_id, a.au_fname, a.au_lname, a.city, a.state
  FROM authors a, publishers p
  WHERE a.city = p.city
    AND a.state = p.state
  ORDER BY a.au_id ASC;
```

The result is:

```
au_id au_fname  au_lname city          state
----- --------- -------- ------------- -----
A03   Hallie    Hull     San Francisco CA
A04   Klee      Hull     San Francisco CA
A05   Christian Kells    New York      NY
```

Tip: JOIN (without CROSS, OUTER, or any other modifiers) is equivalent to INNER JOIN.

The following query uses aggregate functions (Chapter 13) and a GROUP BY clause (Chapter 14) to list the count and total advance paid for each type of book, by publisher.

```
SELECT
    t.type,
    t.pub_id,
    COUNT(r.advance) AS "COUNT(r.advance)",
    SUM(r.advance) AS "SUM(r.advance)"
  FROM royalties r
  INNER JOIN titles t
    ON r.title_id = t.title_id
  WHERE r.advance IS NOT NULL
  GROUP BY t.type, t.pub_id
  ORDER BY t.type ASC, t.pub_id ASC;
```

Using WHERE syntax, the equivalent query is:

```
SELECT
    t.type,
    t.pub_id,
    COUNT(r.advance) AS "COUNT(r.advance)",
    SUM(r.advance) AS "SUM(r.advance)"
  FROM royalties r, titles t
  WHERE r.title_id = t.title_id
    AND r.advance IS NOT NULL
  GROUP BY t.type, t.pub_id
  ORDER BY t.type ASC, t.pub_id ASC;
```

The result is:

```
type       pub_id COUNT(r.advance) SUM(r.advance)
---------- ------ ---------------- --------------
biography  P01                   2       70000.00
biography  P03                   1     1000000.00
children   P04                   2           0.00
computer   P02                   1       15000.00
history    P01                   1       10000.00
history    P03                   2       21000.00
psychology P04                   3      220000.00
```

The following query joins three tables to list the author names and the names of the books that each author wrote (or cowrote).

```
SELECT a.au_fname, a.au_lname, t.title_name
  FROM authors a
  INNER JOIN title_authors ta
    ON a.au_id = ta.au_id
  INNER JOIN titles t
    ON t.title_id = ta.title_id
  ORDER BY a.au_lname ASC, a.au_fname ASC, t.title_name ASC;
```

Using WHERE syntax, the equivalent query is:

```
SELECT a.au_fname, a.au_lname, t.title_name
  FROM authors a, title_authors ta, titles t
  WHERE a.au_id = ta.au_id
    AND t.title_id = ta.title_id
  ORDER BY a.au_lname ASC, a.au_fname ASC, t.title_name ASC;
```

The result is:

```
au_fname  au_lname  title_name
--------- --------- -----------------------------------
Sarah     Buchman   1977!
Sarah     Buchman   200 Years of German Humor
Sarah     Buchman   What Are The Civilian Applications?
Wendy     Heydemark How About Never?
Wendy     Heydemark I Blame My Mother
Wendy     Heydemark Not Without My Faberge Egg
Wendy     Heydemark Spontaneous, Not Annoying
Hallie    Hull      But I Did It Unconsciously
Hallie    Hull      Perhaps It's a Glandular Problem
Klee      Hull      But I Did It Unconsciously
Klee      Hull      Exchange of Platitudes
Klee      Hull      I Blame My Mother
Klee      Hull      Perhaps It's a Glandular Problem
Christian Kells     Ask Your System Administrator
          Kellsey   Just Wait Until After School
          Kellsey   Kiss My Boo-Boo
          Kellsey   Perhaps It's a Glandular Problem
```

Multitable Joins in Microsoft Access

DBMS You can use WHERE syntax or JOIN syntax in **Microsoft Access**, but if you use JOIN syntax in joins that involve three or more tables, you must nest joins by using the following syntax:

```
SELECT columns
  FROM table1
  INNER JOIN (table2 INNER JOIN [(]table3
  [INNER JOIN [(]tableN [INNER JOIN ...)]
  ON table3.column3 op tableN.columnN)]
  ON table2.column2 op table3.column3)
  ON table1.column1 op table2.column2;
```

To run the preceding query in Access, type:

```
SELECT a.au_fname, a.au_lname, t.title_name
  FROM titles AS t
  INNER JOIN (authors AS a
    INNER JOIN title_authors AS ta
      ON a.au_id = ta.au_id)
    ON t.title_id = ta.title_id
  ORDER BY a.au_lname ASC, a.au_fname ASC, t.title_name ASC;
```

The following query uses GROUP BY and HAVING clauses (Chapter 14) to list the number of coauthors of each book written by two or more authors.

```
SELECT
    ta.title_id,
    COUNT(ta.au_id) AS "Num authors"
  FROM authors a
  INNER JOIN title_authors ta
    ON a.au_id = ta.au_id
  GROUP BY ta.title_id
  HAVING COUNT(ta.au_id) > 1
  ORDER BY ta.title_id ASC;
```

Using WHERE syntax, the equivalent query is:

```
SELECT
    ta.title_id,
    COUNT(ta.au_id) AS "Num authors"
  FROM authors a, title_authors ta
  WHERE a.au_id = ta.au_id
  GROUP BY ta.title_id
  HAVING COUNT(ta.au_id) > 1
  ORDER BY ta.title_id ASC;
```

The result is:

```
title_id Num authors
-------- -----------
T04                2
T07                2
T11                3
```

You can also join values in two columns that aren't equal. The following query uses greater-than (>) join to find each book whose revenue (= price × sales) is at least 10 times greater than the advance paid to the author(s). The use of <, <=, >, and >= joins is common, but not-equal joins (<>) are used rarely. Generally, not-equal joins make sense only when used with a self-join (page 122).

```
SELECT t.title_id, t.title_name, r.advance,
    t.price * t.sales AS "Revenue"
  FROM titles t
  INNER JOIN royalties r
    ON t.price * t.sales > r.advance * 10
    AND t.title_id = r.title_id
  ORDER BY t.price * t.sales DESC;
```

Using WHERE syntax, the equivalent query is:

```
SELECT t.title_id, t.title_name, r.advance,
    t.price * t.sales AS "Revenue"
  FROM titles t, royalties r
  WHERE t.price * t.sales > r.advance * 10
    AND t.title_id = r.title_id
  ORDER BY t.price * t.sales DESC;
```

The result is:

title_id	title_name	advance	Revenue
T07	I Blame My Mother	1000000.00	35929790.00
T05	Exchange of Platitudes	100000.00	1400008.00
T12	Spontaneous, Not Annoying	50000.00	1299012.99
T03	Ask Your System Administrator	15000.00	1025396.65
T13	What Are The Civilian Appli...	20000.00	313905.33
T06	How About Never?	20000.00	225834.00
T02	200 Years of German Humor	1000.00	190841.70
T09	Kiss My Boo-Boo	.00	69750.00
T08	Just Wait Until After School	.00	40950.00

The following query calculates the total royalties for all books. The gross royalty of a book is the book's revenue (= sales × price) times the royalty rate (the fraction of revenue paid to the author). In most cases, the author receives an initial advance against royalties. The publisher deducts the advance from the gross royalty to get the net royalty. If the net royalty is positive, the publisher must pay the author; if the net royalty is negative or zero, the author gets nothing, because he or she still hasn't "earned out" the advance. Gross royalties are labeled "Total royalties", gross advances are labeled "Total advances", and net royalties are labeled "Total due to authors".

```
SELECT
    SUM(t.sales * t.price * r.royalty_rate)
      AS "Total royalties",
    SUM(r.advance) AS "Total advances",
    SUM((t.sales * t.price * r.royalty_rate) - r.advance)
      AS "Total due to authors"
  FROM titles t
  INNER JOIN royalties r
    ON r.title_id = t.title_id
  WHERE t.sales IS NOT NULL;
```

Using WHERE syntax, the equivalent query is:

```
SELECT
    SUM(t.sales * t.price * r.royalty_rate)
      AS "Total royalties",
    SUM(r.advance) AS "Total advances",
    SUM((t.sales * t.price * r.royalty_rate) - r.advance)
      AS "Total due to authors"
  FROM titles t, royalties r
  WHERE r.title_id = t.title_id
    AND t.sales IS NOT NULL;
```

The result is:

```
Total royalties Total advances Total due to authors
--------------- -------------- --------------------
     4387219.55     1336000.00           3051219.55
```

Creating Outer Joins with OUTER JOIN

In the preceding section, you learned that inner joins return rows only if at least one row from both tables satisfies the join condition(s). An inner join eliminates the rows that don't match with a row from the other table, whereas an **outer join** returns *all* rows from at least one of the tables (provided that those rows meet any WHERE or HAVING search conditions).

Outer joins are useful for answering questions that involve missing quantities: authors who have written no books or classes with no enrolled students, for example. Outer joins also are helpful for creating reports in which you want to list all the rows of one table along with matching rows from another table: all authors and any books that sold more than a given number of copies, for example, or all products with order quantities, including products no one ordered.

Unlike other joins, the order in which you specify the tables in outer joins is important, so the two join operands are called the **left table** and the **right table**. Outer joins come in three flavors:

- **Left outer join**. The result of a left outer join includes all the rows from the left table specified in the LEFT OUTER JOIN clause, not just the rows in which the joined columns match. If a row in the left table has no matching rows in the right table, the associated row in the result contains nulls for all SELECT-clause columns coming from the right table.
- **Right outer join**. A right outer join is the reverse of a left outer join. All rows from the right table are returned. Nulls are returned for the left table if a right-table row has no matching row in the left table.
- **Full outer join**. A full outer join, which is a combination of left and right outer joins, returns all rows in both the left and right tables. If a row has no match in the other table, the SELECT-clause columns from the other table contain nulls. If a match occurs between the tables, the entire row in the result contains data values from both tables.

To summarize, all rows are retrieved from the left table referenced in a left outer join, all rows are retrieved from the right table referenced in a right outer join, and all rows from both tables are retrieved in a full outer join. In all cases, unmatched rows are padded with nulls (page 22). In the result, you can't distinguish the nulls (if any) that were in the input tables originally from the nulls inserted by the outer-join operation. Remember that the conditions NULL = NULL and NULL = *any_value* are unknown and not matches.

For outer joins, you should use JOIN syntax instead of WHERE syntax when possible, because JOIN syntax is more precise. SQL lacks standardized WHERE syntax for outer joins, so syntax varies by DBMS. A DBMS also might place restrictions on WHERE outer joins that don't exist for JOIN outer joins. See the DBMS tip later in this section for specific information.

Be wary of the order in which tables appear in outer joins. Unlike other joins, outer joins aren't **associative**—that is, the result of a query that involves an outer join depends on the order in which the tables are grouped and joined (associated). The following two three-table inner joins are equivalent (except for the column order in the result):

```
SELECT * FROM table1
  INNER JOIN table2
  INNER JOIN table3
```

and:

```
SELECT * FROM table2
  INNER JOIN table3
  INNER JOIN table1
```

But the following three-table outer joins yield different results:

```
SELECT * FROM table1
  LEFT OUTER JOIN table2
  LEFT OUTER JOIN table3
```

and:

```
SELECT * FROM table2
  LEFT OUTER JOIN table3
  LEFT OUTER JOIN table1
```

DBMS **Microsoft SQL Server** supports the standard OUTER JOIN syntax but older versions use the (nonstandard) outer join operator * in WHERE syntax to create outer joins. Attach * to the left or right of the comparison operator to create a left or right outer join. For outer joins, WHERE syntax is less precise than OUTER JOIN syntax and can yield an ambiguous query. The *= and =* outer-join operators are deprecated (slated for extinction) in newer versions of SQL Server.

Oracle 8i and earlier don't support JOIN syntax; use WHERE joins instead. Oracle 9i and later support the standard OUTER JOIN syntax. In WHERE syntax, Oracle uses the (nonstandard) outer join operator (+) to create outer joins. Add (+) after the table that must be expanded (filled with nulls).

The following query uses a left outer join to include all authors in the result, regardless of whether a publisher is located in the same city.

```
SELECT a.au_fname, a.au_lname, p.pub_name
  FROM authors a
  LEFT OUTER JOIN publishers p
    ON a.city = p.city
  ORDER BY p.pub_name ASC, a.au_lname ASC, a.au_fname ASC;
```

In the following result, note that there's no matching data for four of the listed authors, so these rows contain null in the column *pub_name*.

```
au_fname  au_lname    pub_name
--------- ----------- -----------------
Sarah     Buchman     NULL
Wendy     Heydemark   NULL
          Kellsey     NULL
Paddy     O'Furniture NULL
Christian Kells       Abatis Publishers
Hallie    Hull        Core Dump Books
Klee      Hull        Core Dump Books
```

DBMS To run the preceding query in older versions of **Microsoft SQL Server** by using WHERE syntax, type:

```
SELECT a.au_fname, a.au_lname, p.pub_name
  FROM authors a, publishers p
  WHERE a.city *= p.city
  ORDER BY p.pub_name ASC, a.au_lname ASC, a.au_fname ASC;
```

To run the preceding query in **Oracle** 8i or earlier, type:

```
SELECT a.au_fname, a.au_lname, p.pub_name
  FROM authors a, publishers p
  WHERE a.city = p.city (+)
  ORDER BY p.pub_name ASC, a.au_lname ASC, a.au_fname ASC;
```

The following query uses a right outer join to include all publishers in the result, regardless of whether an author lives in the publisher's city.

```
SELECT a.au_fname, a.au_lname, p.pub_name
  FROM authors a
  RIGHT OUTER JOIN publishers p
    ON a.city = p.city
  ORDER BY p.pub_name ASC, a.au_lname ASC, a.au_fname ASC;
```

In the following result, note that there's no matching data for two of the listed publishers, so these rows contain nulls in the columns *au_fname* and *au_lname*.

```
au_fname  au_lname pub_name
--------- -------- -------------------
Christian Kells    Abatis Publishers
Hallie    Hull     Core Dump Books
Klee      Hull     Core Dump Books
NULL      NULL     Schadenfreude Press
NULL      NULL     Tenterhooks Press
```

DBMS To run the preceding query in older versions of **Microsoft SQL Server** by using WHERE syntax, type:

```
SELECT a.au_fname, a.au_lname, p.pub_name
  FROM authors a, publishers p
  WHERE a.city =* p.city
  ORDER BY p.pub_name ASC, a.au_lname ASC, a.au_fname ASC;
```

To run the preceding query in **Oracle** 8i or earlier, type:

```
SELECT a.au_fname, a.au_lname, p.pub_name
  FROM authors a, publishers p
  WHERE a.city (+) = p.city
  ORDER BY p.pub_name ASC, a.au_lname ASC, a.au_fname ASC;
```

The following query uses a full outer join to include all publishers and all authors in the result, regardless of whether a publisher and author are located in the same city.

```
SELECT a.au_fname, a.au_lname, p.pub_name
  FROM authors a
  FULL OUTER JOIN publishers p
    ON a.city = p.city
  ORDER BY p.pub_name ASC, a.au_lname ASC, a.au_fname ASC;
```

The following result contains nine rows: four rows for authors who have no matching rows in the table *publishers*, three rows in which the author and publisher coexist in the same city, and two rows for publishers who have no matching city in the table *authors*.

```
au_fname  au_lname    pub_name
--------- ----------- -------------------
Sarah     Buchman     NULL
Wendy     Heydemark   NULL
          Kellsey     NULL
Paddy     O'Furniture NULL
Christian Kells       Abatis Publishers
Hallie    Hull        Core Dump Books
Klee      Hull        Core Dump Books
NULL      NULL        Schadenfreude Press
NULL      NULL        Tenterhooks Press
```

DBMS In older versions of **Microsoft SQL Server**, you can't place the * operator on both sides of the comparison operator to form a full outer join. Instead, form the union (Chapter 18) of a left and right outer join. To run the preceding query by using WHERE syntax, type:

```
SELECT a.au_fname, a.au_lname, p.pub_name
  FROM authors a, publishers p
  WHERE a.city *= p.city
UNION ALL
SELECT a.au_fname, a.au_lname, p.pub_name
  FROM authors a, publishers p
  WHERE a.city =* p.city
    AND a.city IS NULL;
```

In **Oracle**, you can't place the (+) operator on both sides of the comparison operator to form a full outer join. Instead, form the union (Chapter 18) of a left and right outer join. To run the preceding query in Oracle 8i or earlier, type:

```
SELECT a.au_fname, a.au_lname, p.pub_name
  FROM authors a, publishers p
  WHERE a.city = p.city (+)
UNION ALL
SELECT a.au_fname, a.au_lname, p.pub_name
  FROM authors a, publishers p
  WHERE a.city (+) = p.city
    AND a.city IS NULL;
```

Microsoft Access and **MySQL** don't support full outer joins, but you can replicate one by taking the union (Chapter 18) of left and right outer joins. In the following example, the first UNION table is a left outer join restricted to return all the rows in *authors* as well as the matched rows in *publishers* based on *city*. The second UNION table is a right outer join restricted to return only the unmatched rows in *publishers*. To run the preceding query, type:

```
SELECT a.au_fname, a.au_lname, p.pub_name
  FROM authors a
  LEFT OUTER JOIN publishers p
    ON a.city = p.city
UNION ALL
SELECT a.au_fname, a.au_lname, p.pub_name
  FROM authors a
  RIGHT OUTER JOIN publishers p
    ON a.city = p.city
  WHERE a.city IS NULL;
```

Creating a Self-Join

A **self-join** is a normal SQL join that joins a table to itself and retrieves rows from a table by comparing values in one or more columns in the same table. Self-joins often are used in tables with a **reflexive relationship**, which is a primary-key/foreign-key relationship from a column or combination of columns in a table to other columns in that same table. For information about keys, see Chapter 2.

Suppose that you have the following table, named *employees*:

```
emp_id emp_name          boss_id
------ ----------------- -------
E01    Lord Copper       NULL
E02    Jocelyn Hitchcock E01
E03    Mr. Salter        E01
E04    William Boot      E03
E05    Mr. Corker        E03
```

emp_id is a primary key that uniquely identifies the employee, and *boss_id* is an employee ID that identifies the employee's manager. Each manager also is an employee, so to ensure that each manager ID that is added to the table matches an existing employee ID, *boss_id* is defined as a foreign key of *emp_id*. The following query uses this reflexive relationship to compare rows within the table and retrieve the *name* of the manager of each employee. (You wouldn't need a join at all to get just the manager's ID.)

```
SELECT
    e1.emp_name AS "Employee name",
    e2.emp_name AS "Boss name"
  FROM employees e1
  INNER JOIN employees e2
    ON e1.boss_id = e2.emp_id;
```

In the following result, note that Lord Copper, who has no boss, is excluded from the result because his null *boss_id* doesn't satisfy the join condition.

```
Employee name     Boss name
----------------- -----------
Jocelyn Hitchcock Lord Copper
Mr. Salter        Lord Copper
William Boot      Mr. Salter
Mr. Corker        Mr. Salter
```

The same table (*employees*) appears twice in the preceding query with two different aliases (*e1* and *e2*) that are used to qualify column names in the join condition:

```
e1.boss_id = e2.emp_id
```

As with any join, a self-join requires two tables, but instead of adding a second table to the join, you add a second **instance** of the same table. That way, you can compare a column in the first instance of the table to a column in the second instance. As with all joins, the DBMS combines and returns rows of the table that satisfy the join condition. You really aren't creating another copy of the table—you're joining the table to itself—but the effect might be easier to understand if you think about it as being two tables.

Tip: You can join a table to itself even if no reflexive relationship exists. A common type of self-join compares a column in the first instance of the table to the *same* column in the second instance. This join condition lets you compare the values in a column to one another, as shown in the subsequent examples in this section.

The following query uses a WHERE search condition and self-join from the column *state* to itself to find all authors who live in the same state as author A04 (Klee Hull).

```
SELECT a1.au_id, a1.au_fname, a1.au_lname, a1.state
  FROM authors a1
  INNER JOIN authors a2
    ON a1.state = a2.state
  WHERE a2.au_id = 'A04';
```

Using WHERE syntax, the equivalent query is:

```
SELECT a1.au_id, a1.au_fname, a1.au_lname, a1.state
  FROM authors a1, authors a2
  WHERE a1.state = a2.state
    AND a2.au_id = 'A04';
```

The result is:

```
au_id au_fname au_lname state
----- -------- -------- -----
A03   Hallie   Hull     CA
A04   Klee     Hull     CA
A06            Kellsey  CA
```

Self-joins can often be restated as subqueries (Chapter 17). Using a subquery, the preceding query is equivalent to:

```
SELECT au_id, au_fname, au_lname, state
  FROM authors
  WHERE state IN
    (SELECT state
       FROM authors
       WHERE au_id = 'A04');
```

For every biography, the following query lists the other biographies that outsold it. Note that the WHERE search condition requires *type = 'biography'* for both tables *t1* and *t2* because the join condition considers the column *type* to be two separate columns.

```
SELECT t1.title_id, t1.sales,
    t2.title_id AS "Better seller",
    t2.sales AS "Higher sales"
  FROM titles t1
  INNER JOIN titles t2
    ON t1.sales < t2.sales
  WHERE t1.type = 'biography'
    AND t2.type = 'biography'
  ORDER BY t1.title_id ASC, t2.sales ASC;
```

Using WHERE syntax, the equivalent query is:

```
SELECT t1.title_id, t1.sales,
    t2.title_id AS "Better seller",
    t2.sales AS "Higher sales"
  FROM titles t1, titles t2
  WHERE t1.sales < t2.sales
    AND t1.type = 'biography'
    AND t2.type = 'biography'
  ORDER BY t1.title_id ASC, t2.sales ASC;
```

```
The result is:

title_id sales  Better seller Higher sales
-------- ------ ------------- ------------
T06       11320 T12                 100001
T06       11320 T07                1500200
T12      100001 T07                1500200
```

CHAPTER 17

Subqueries

Understanding Subqueries

To this point, I've used a single SELECT statement to retrieve data from one or more tables. This chapter describes nested queries, which let you retrieve or modify data based on another query's result.

A **subquery**, or **subselect**, is a SELECT statement embedded in another SQL statement. You can nest a subquery in:

- The SELECT, FROM, WHERE, or HAVING clause of a SELECT statement
- Another subquery
- An INSERT, UPDATE, or DELETE statement (Chapters 19 and 20)

In general, you can use a subquery anywhere an expression is allowed, but your DBMS might restrict where they can appear.

Suppose that you want to list the names of the publishers of biographies. The naive approach is to write two queries: one query to retrieve the IDs of all the biography publishers:

```
SELECT pub_id
  FROM titles
  WHERE type = 'biography';
```

The result is:

```
pub_id
------
P01
P03
P01
P01
```

And a second query that uses the first query's result to list the publisher names:

```
SELECT pub_name
  FROM publishers
  WHERE pub_id IN ('P01', 'P03');
```

The result is:

```
pub_name
-------------------
Abatis Publishers
Schadenfreude Press
```

A better way is to use an inner join (page 109):

```
SELECT DISTINCT pub_name
  FROM publishers p
  INNER JOIN titles t
    ON p.pub_id = t.pub_id
  WHERE t.type = 'biography';
```

Another alternative is to use a subquery:

```
SELECT pub_name
  FROM publishers
  WHERE pub_id IN
    (SELECT pub_id
       FROM titles
       WHERE type = 'biography');
```

The subquery in the preceding example is highlighted in bold. A subquery also is called an **inner query**, and the statement containing a subquery is called an **outer query**. In other words, an enclosed subquery is an inner query of an outer query. Remember that a subquery can be nested in another subquery, so *inner* and *outer* are relative terms in statements with multiple nested subqueries.

The DBMS processes the inner query (bold text) first and then uses its interim result to run the outer query (plain text) and get the final result. The IN keyword that introduces the subquery tests for list membership and works like IN in "List Filtering with IN" on page 59.

DBMS **MySQL** 4.1 and later support subqueries, but earlier versions don't. You can't run the examples in this chapter if you're using MySQL 4.0 or earlier.

Subquery Syntax

The syntax of a subquery is the same as that of a normal SELECT statement (page 25) except for the following differences:

- You can nest a subquery in a SELECT, FROM, WHERE, or HAVING clause or in another subquery.
- Always enclose a subquery in parentheses.
- Don't terminate a subquery with a semicolon. (You still must terminate the statement that contains the subquery with a semicolon.)
- Don't put an ORDER BY clause in a subquery. (A subquery returns an intermediate result that you never see, so sorting a subquery makes no sense.)
- A subquery is a single SELECT statement. (You can't use, say, a UNION of multiple SELECT statements as a subquery.)
- A subquery can use columns in the tables listed in its own FROM clause or in the outer query's FROM clause.
- If a table appears in an inner query but not in the outer query, you can't include that table's columns in the final result (that is, in the outer query's SELECT clause).
- Depending on the context in which it's used, a subquery might be required to return a limited number of rows or columns. A subquery that returns one row and one column (a single value) is called a **scalar subquery**. A subquery can also return an empty table (zero rows).

In practice, a subquery usually appears in a WHERE clause that takes one of these forms:

- WHERE *test_expr op* (*subquery*)
- WHERE *test_expr* [NOT] IN (*subquery*)
- WHERE *test_expr op* ALL (*subquery*)
- WHERE *test_expr op* ANY (*subquery*)
- WHERE [NOT] EXISTS (*subquery*)

test_expr is a literal value, a column name, an expression, or a scalar subquery; *op* is a comparison operator (=, <>, <, <=, >, or >=); and *subquery* is a subquery. You can use these subquery forms in a HAVING clause, too.

DBMS The SQL standard doesn't specify a maximum number of subquery nesting levels, so your DBMS will set its own upper limit. This built-in limit typically exceeds the limit of human comprehension. **Microsoft SQL Server**, for example, allows 32 levels of nesting.

Subqueries vs. Joins

The examples in "Understanding Subqueries" earlier in this chapter showed two equivalent queries: one used a join, and the other used a subquery. Many subqueries can be formulated alternatively as joins. In fact, a subquery is a way to relate one table to another without actually doing a join.

Because subqueries can be hard to use and debug, you might prefer to use joins, but you can pose some questions only as subqueries. In cases where you can use subqueries and joins interchangeably, you should test queries on your DBMS to see whether a performance difference exists between a statement that uses a subquery and a semantically equivalent version that uses a join. For example, the query

```
SELECT MAX(table1.col1)
  FROM table1
  WHERE table1.col1 IN
    (SELECT table2.col1
       FROM table2);
```

usually will run faster than

```
SELECT MAX(table1.col1)
  FROM table1
  INNER JOIN table2
    ON table1.col1 = table2.col1;
```

The following syntax diagrams and examples show some equivalent statements that use subqueries and joins.

The IN subquery:

```
SELECT *
  FROM table1
  WHERE id IN (SELECT id FROM table2);
```

is equivalent to the inner join:

```
SELECT DISTINCT table1.*
  FROM table1
  INNER JOIN table2
    ON table1.id = table2.id;
```

For example, the following two queries are equivalent:

```
SELECT au_id, city
  FROM authors
  WHERE city IN (SELECT city FROM publishers);
```

```
SELECT DISTINCT a.au_id, a.city
  FROM authors a
  INNER JOIN publishers p
    ON a.city = p.city;
```

The result (of either statement) lists the authors who live in the same city in which a publisher is located:

```
au_id city
----- -------------
A03   San Francisco
A04   San Francisco
A05   New York
```

The NOT IN subquery:

```
SELECT *
  FROM table1
  WHERE id NOT IN (SELECT id FROM table2);
```

is equivalent to the left outer join:

```
SELECT table1.*
  FROM table1
  LEFT OUTER JOIN table2
    ON table1.id = table2.id
  WHERE table2.id IS NULL;
```

For example, the following two queries are equivalent:

```
SELECT au_id, au_fname, au_lname
  FROM authors
  WHERE au_id NOT IN (SELECT au_id FROM title_authors);
```

```
SELECT a.au_id, a.au_fname, a.au_lname
  FROM authors a
  LEFT OUTER JOIN title_authors ta
    ON a.au_id = ta.au_id
  WHERE ta.au_id IS NULL;
```

The result (of either statement) lists the authors who haven't written (or cowritten) a book:

```
au_id au_fname au_lname
----- -------- -----------
A07   Paddy    O'Furniture
```

You also can write a self-join (page 122) as a subquery. For example, the following two queries are equivalent:

```
SELECT au_id, au_fname, au_lname, state
  FROM authors
  WHERE state IN
    (SELECT state
       FROM authors
       WHERE au_id = 'A04');
```

```
SELECT a1.au_id, a1.au_fname, a1.au_lname, a1.state
  FROM authors a1
  INNER JOIN authors a2
    ON a1.state = a2.state
  WHERE a2.au_id = 'A04';
```

The result (of either statement) lists the authors who live in the same state as author A04 (Klee Hull):

```
au_id au_fname au_lname state
----- -------- -------- -----
A03   Hallie   Hull     CA
A04   Klee     Hull     CA
A06            Kellsey  CA
```

Favor subqueries if you're comparing an aggregate value (Chapter 13) to other values. For example, the following query lists all books whose price equals the highest book price:

```
SELECT title_id, price
  FROM titles
  WHERE price = (SELECT MAX(price) FROM titles);
```

The result is:

```
title_id price
-------- -----
T03      39.95
```

Without a subquery, you'd need two SELECT statements to list all the books with the highest price: one query to find the highest price and a second query to list all the books selling for that price.

Use joins when you include columns from multiple tables in the result. For example, the following query lists the authors who live in the same city in which a publisher is located, and includes the publisher in the result:

```
SELECT a.au_id, a.city, p.pub_id
  FROM authors a
  INNER JOIN publishers p
    ON a.city = p.city;
```

The result is:

```
au_id city          pub_id
----- ------------- ------
A03   San Francisco P02
A04   San Francisco P02
A05   New York      P01
```

You can't accomplish this same task with a subquery, because it's illegal to include a column in the outer query's SELECT-clause list from a table that appears in only the inner query:

```
SELECT a.au_id, a.city, p.pub_id                          --Illegal
  FROM authors a
  WHERE a.city IN (SELECT p.city FROM publishers p);
```

Tip: You always can express an inner join as a subquery, but not vice versa. This asymmetry occurs because inner joins are commutative; you can join tables A to B in either order and get the same answer. Subqueries lack this property. (You always can express an outer join as a subquery, too, even though outer joins aren't commutative.)

Qualifying Column Names in Subqueries

Recall from "Qualifying Column Names" on page 98 that you can qualify a column name explicitly with a table name to identify the column unambiguously. In statements that contain subqueries, column names are qualified implicitly by the table referenced in the FROM clause at the same nesting level.

In the following query, the tables *publishers* and *titles* both contain a column named *pub_id*, but you don't have to qualify *pub_id* in this query because of the implicit assumptions about table names that SQL makes.

```
SELECT pub_name
  FROM publishers
  WHERE pub_id IN
    (SELECT pub_id FROM titles WHERE type = 'biography');
```

The column names are qualified implicitly, meaning:

- The column *pub_id* in the outer query's WHERE clause is qualified implicitly by the table *publishers* in the outer query's FROM clause.
- The column *pub_id* in the subquery's SELECT clause is qualified implicitly by the table *titles* in the subquery's FROM clause.

The equivalent query, but with explicit qualification of *pub_id*, is:

```
SELECT pub_name
  FROM publishers
  WHERE publishers.pub_id IN
    (SELECT titles.pub_id
       FROM titles
       WHERE type = 'biography');
```

The result (of either statement) lists the names of biography publishers:

```
pub_name
-------------------
Abatis Publishers
Schadenfreude Press
```

You can use explicit qualifiers to override SQL's default assumptions about table names and specify that a column is to match a table at a nesting level outside the column's own level.

If a column name can match more than one table at the same nesting level, the column name is ambiguous, and you must qualify it with a table name (or table alias).

Using Subqueries as Column Expressions

In earlier chapters, you learned that the items in a SELECT-clause list can be literals, column names, or more-complex expressions. SQL also lets you to embed a subquery in a SELECT-clause list.

A subquery that's used as a column expression must be a scalar subquery. Recall that a scalar subquery returns a single value (that is, a one-row, one-column result). In most cases, you'll have to use an aggregate function (Chapter 13) or restrictive WHERE conditions in the subquery to guarantee that the subquery returns only one row.

The syntax for the SELECT-clause list is the same as you've been using all along, except that you can specify a parenthesized subquery as one of the column expressions in the list.

The following query uses two simple subqueries as column expressions to list each biography, its price, the average price of all books (not just biographies), and the difference between the price of the biography and the average price of all books. The aggregate function AVG() guarantees that each subquery returns a single value. Remember that AVG() ignores nulls (page 22) when computing an average.

```
SELECT title_id, price,
    (SELECT AVG(price) FROM titles) AS "AVG(price)",
    price - (SELECT AVG(price) FROM titles) AS "Difference"
  FROM titles
  WHERE type='biography';
```

The result is:

```
title_id price   AVG(price) Difference
-------- ------- ---------- ----------
T06        19.95    18.3875     1.5625
T07        23.95    18.3875     5.5625
T10         NULL    18.3875       NULL
T12        12.99    18.3875    -5.3975
```

DBMS In **Microsoft Access**, you must increase the precision of the average-price calculation in the preceding example. Use the type-conversion function CDbl() to coerce the average price to a double-precision floating-point number. To run the preceding query, change both occurrences of AVG(price) to CDbl(AVG(price)). For details, see the DBMS tip in “Converting Data Types” in Chapter 11.

You also can use a subquery in a FROM clause. The following query uses a FROM subquery to calculate the greatest number of titles written (or co-written) by any author. Note that the outer query uses a table alias (*ta*) and column alias (*count_titles*) to reference the inner query's result.

```
SELECT MAX(ta.count_titles) AS "Max titles"
  FROM (SELECT COUNT(*) AS count_titles
          FROM title_authors
          GROUP BY au_id) ta;
```

The result is:

```
Max titles
----------
         4
```

Comparing a Subquery Value by Using a Comparison Operator

You can use a subquery as a filter in a WHERE clause or HAVING clause by using one of the comparison operators (=, <>, <, <=, >, or >=).

- The comparison operators (page 40) work the same way as they do in other comparisons.
- The subquery's SELECT-clause list can include only one expression or column name.
- The compared values must have the same data type or must be implicitly convertible to the same type (page 77).
- String comparisons are case insensitive or case sensitive, depending on your DBMS.
- The subquery must return a single value (a one-row, one-column result). A subquery that returns more than one value will cause an error.
- If the subquery result contains zero rows, the comparison test will evaluate to false.

The hard part of writing these statements is getting the subquery to return one value, which you can guarantee several ways:

- Using an aggregate function (Chapter 13) on an ungrouped table always returns a single value.
- Using a join with the outer query based on a key (page 11) always returns a single value.

The following query tests the result of a subquery for equality to list the authors who live in the state in which Tenterhooks Press is located. Only one publisher is named Tenterhooks Press, so the inner WHERE condition guarantees that the inner query returns a single-valued result.

```
SELECT au_id, au_fname, au_lname, state
  FROM authors
  WHERE state =
    (SELECT state
       FROM publishers
       WHERE pub_name = 'Tenterhooks Press');
```

The result is:

```
au_id au_fname au_lname state
----- -------- -------- -----
A03   Hallie   Hull     CA
A04   Klee     Hull     CA
A06            Kellsey  CA
```

The following query lists the books with above-average sales. Subqueries introduced with comparison operators often use aggregate functions to return a single value.

```
SELECT title_id, sales
  FROM titles
  WHERE sales > (SELECT AVG(sales) FROM titles);
```

The result is:

```
title_id sales
-------- -------
T05       201440
T07      1500200
```

The following query uses a subquery in a HAVING clause to list the publishers whose average sales exceed overall average sales. Again, the subquery returns a single value (the average of all sales).

```
SELECT pub_id, AVG(sales) AS "AVG(sales)"
  FROM titles
  GROUP BY pub_id
  HAVING AVG(sales) > (SELECT AVG(sales) FROM titles);
```

The result is:

```
pub_id AVG(sales)
------ ----------
P03     506744.33
```

Testing Set Membership with IN

"List Filtering with IN" on page 59 describes how to use the IN keyword in a WHERE clause to compare a literal, column value, or more-complex expression to a list of values. You also can use a subquery to generate the list.

- IN works the same way with the values in a subquery result as it does with a parenthesized list of values (page 59).
- The subquery's SELECT-clause list can include only one expression or column name.
- The compared values must have the same data type or must be implicitly convertible to the same type (page 77).
- String comparisons are case insensitive or case sensitive, depending on your DBMS.
- The subquery must return exactly one column and zero or more rows. A subquery that returns more than one column will cause an error.
- To reverse the effect of the IN test, use NOT IN.

The following query lists the names of the publishers that have published biographies. The DBMS evaluates this statement in two steps. First, the inner query returns the IDs of the publishers that have published biographies (P01 and P03). Second, the DBMS substitutes these values into the outer query, which finds the names that go with the IDs in the table *publishers*.

```
SELECT pub_name
  FROM publishers
  WHERE pub_id IN
    (SELECT pub_id FROM titles WHERE type = 'biography');
```

The result is:

```
pub_name
-------------------
Abatis Publishers
Schadenfreude Press
```

To list publishers that *haven't* published biographies, use NOT IN:

```
SELECT pub_name
  FROM publishers
  WHERE pub_id NOT IN
    (SELECT pub_id FROM titles WHERE type = 'biography');
```

The following query lists the names of the authors who have published a book with publisher P03 (Schadenfreude Press). The join to the table *authors* is necessary to include the authors' names (not just their IDs) in the result.

```
SELECT DISTINCT a.au_id, au_fname, au_lname
  FROM title_authors ta
  INNER JOIN authors a
    ON ta.au_id = a.au_id
  WHERE title_id IN
    (SELECT title_id FROM titles WHERE pub_id = 'P03');
```

The result is:

```
au_id au_fname au_lname
----- -------- ---------
A01   Sarah    Buchman
A02   Wendy    Heydemark
A04   Klee     Hull
```

A subquery can itself include one or more subqueries. The following query lists the names of authors who have participated in writing at least one biography. The innermost query returns the title IDs T06, T07, T10, and T12. The DBMS evaluates the subquery at the next higher level by using these title IDs and returns the author IDs. Finally, the outermost query uses the author IDs to find the names of the authors.

```
SELECT au_id, au_fname, au_lname
  FROM authors
  WHERE au_id IN
    (SELECT au_id
       FROM title_authors
       WHERE title_id IN
         (SELECT title_id
            FROM titles
            WHERE type = 'biography'));
```

The result is:

```
au_id au_fname au_lname
----- -------- ---------
A02   Wendy    Heydemark
A04   Klee     Hull
```

Tip: IN is equivalent to =ANY (page 140). NOT IN is equivalent to <>ALL (page 138).

Comparing All Subquery Values with ALL

You can use the ALL keyword to determine whether a value is less than or greater than *all* the values in a subquery result.

- ALL modifies a comparison operator in a subquery comparison test (page 134) and follows =, <>, <, <=, >, or >=.
- The combination of a comparison operator and ALL tells the DBMS how to apply the comparison test to the values returned by a subquery. <ALL, for example, means less than every value in the subquery result, and >ALL means greater than every value in the subquery result.
- When ALL is used with <, <=, >, or >=, the comparison is equivalent to evaluating the subquery result's minimum or maximum value. <ALL means less than every subquery value—in other words, less than the minimum value. >ALL means greater than every subquery value—that is, greater than the maximum value.
- Semantic equivalence doesn't mean that two queries will *run* at the same speed. For example, the query

  ```
  SELECT * FROM table1
    WHERE col1 > ANY (SELECT MAX(col1) FROM table2);
  ```

  usually is faster than

  ```
  SELECT * FROM table1
    WHERE col1 > ALL (SELECT col1 FROM table2);
  ```

- The comparison =ALL is valid but isn't often used. =ALL always will be false unless all the values returned by the subquery are identical (and equal to the test value).
- The subquery's SELECT-clause list can include only one expression or column name.
- The compared values must have the same data type or must be implicitly convertible to the same type (page 77).
- String comparisons are case insensitive or case sensitive, depending on your DBMS.
- The subquery must return exactly one column and zero or more rows. A subquery that returns more than one column will cause an error.
- If the subquery returns no rows, the ALL condition is true. (You might find this result to be counterintuitive.)

The following query lists the authors who live in a city in which no publisher is located. The inner query finds all the cities in which publishers are located, and the outer query compares each author's city to all the publishers' cities.

```
SELECT au_id, au_lname, au_fname, city
  FROM authors
  WHERE city <> ALL
    (SELECT city
       FROM publishers);
```

The result is:

```
au_id au_lname    au_fname city
----- ----------- -------- ---------
A01   Buchman     Sarah    Bronx
A02   Heydemark   Wendy    Boulder
A06   Kellsey              Palo Alto
A07   O'Furniture Paddy    Sarasota
```

Tip: <>ALL is equivalent to NOT IN (page 136).

The following query lists the nonbiographies that are priced less than all the biographies. The inner query finds all the biography prices. The outer query inspects the lowest price in the list and determines whether each non-biography is cheaper. The *price IS NOT NULL* condition is required because the price of biography T10 is null. Without this condition, the entire query would return zero rows, because it's impossible to determine whether a price is less than null (page 22).

```
SELECT title_id, title_name
  FROM titles
  WHERE type <> 'biography'
    AND price < ALL
      (SELECT price
         FROM titles
         WHERE type = 'biography'
           AND price IS NOT NULL);
```

The result is:

```
title_id title_name
-------- --------------------------------
T05      Exchange of Platitudes
T08      Just Wait Until After School
T11      Perhaps It's a Glandular Problem
```

Comparing Some Subquery Values with ANY

ANY works like ALL but instead determines whether a value is equal to, less than, or greater than *any* (at least one) of the values in a subquery result.

- ANY modifies a comparison operator in a subquery comparison test (page 134) and follows =, <>, <, <=, >, or >=.
- The combination of a comparison operator and ANY tells the DBMS how to apply the comparison test to the values returned by a subquery. <ANY, for example, means less than at least one value in the subquery result, and >ANY means greater than at least one value in the subquery result.
- When ANY is used with <, <=, >, or >=, the comparison is equivalent to evaluating the subquery result's maximum or minimum value. <ANY means less than at least one subquery value—in other words, less than the maximum value. >ANY means greater than at least one subquery value—that is, greater than the minimum value.
- The subquery's SELECT-clause list can include only one expression or column name.
- The compared values must have the same data type or must be implicitly convertible to the same type (page 77).
- String comparisons are case insensitive or case sensitive, depending on your DBMS.
- The subquery must return exactly one column and zero or more rows. A subquery that returns more than one column will cause an error.
- If the subquery returns no rows, the ANY condition is false.

The following query lists the authors who live in a city in which a publisher is located. The inner query finds all the cities in which publishers are located, and the outer query compares each author's city to all the publishers' cities.

```
SELECT au_id, au_lname, au_fname, city
  FROM authors
  WHERE city = ANY (SELECT city FROM publishers);
```

The result is:

```
au_id au_lname au_fname  city
----- -------- --------- -------------
A03   Hull     Hallie    San Francisco
A04   Hull     Klee      San Francisco
A05   Kells    Christian New York
```

Tip: =ANY is equivalent to IN (page 136).

The following query lists the nonbiographies that are priced less than at least one biography. The inner query finds all the biography prices. The outer query inspects the highest price in the list and determines whether each nonbiography is cheaper.

Unlike the <ALL comparison in the preceding section, the *price IS NOT NULL* condition isn't required here, even though the price of biography T10 is null. The DBMS doesn't determine whether all the price comparisons are true—just whether at least one is true—so the null comparison is ignored.

```
SELECT title_id, title_name
  FROM titles
  WHERE type <> 'biography'
    AND price < ANY
      (SELECT price FROM titles WHERE type = 'biography');
```

The result is:

```
title_id title_name
-------- --------------------------------
T01      1977!
T02      200 Years of German Humor
T04      But I Did It Unconsciously
T05      Exchange of Platitudes
T08      Just Wait Until After School
T09      Kiss My Boo-Boo
T11      Perhaps It's a Glandular Problem
```

The following query lists the books that outsold at least one of the books that author A06 wrote (or cowrote). The inner query uses a join to find the sales of each book by author A06. The outer query inspects the lowest sales figure in the list and determines whether each book sold more copies. Again, the IS NOT NULL condition isn't needed here.

```
SELECT title_id, title_name
  FROM titles
  WHERE sales > ANY
    (SELECT sales
       FROM title_authors ta
       INNER JOIN titles t
         ON t.title_id = ta.title_id
       WHERE ta.au_id = 'A06');
```

Testing Existence with EXISTS

So far in this chapter, I've been using the comparison operators IN, ALL, and ANY to compare a specific test value to values in a subquery result. EXISTS and NOT EXISTS don't compare values; rather, they simply look for the existence or nonexistence of rows in a subquery result.

- An existence test doesn't compare values, so it isn't preceded by a test expression.
- The subquery can return any number of columns and rows.
- By convention, the SELECT clause in the subquery is SELECT * to retrieve all columns. Listing specific column names is unnecessary, because EXISTS simply tests for the *existence* of rows that satisfy the subquery conditions; the actual values in the rows are irrelevant.
- All IN, ALL, and ANY queries can be expressed with EXISTS or NOT EXISTS.
- If the subquery returns at least one row, an EXISTS test is true, and a NOT EXISTS test is false.
- If the subquery returns no rows, an EXISTS test is false, and a NOT EXISTS test is true.
- A subquery row that contains only nulls counts as a row. (An EXISTS test is true, and a NOT EXISTS test is false.)
- Because an EXISTS test performs no comparisons, it's not subject to the same problems with nulls (page 22) as tests that use IN, ALL, or ANY.

The following query lists the names of the publishers that have published biographies. This query considers each publisher's ID in turn and determines whether it causes the existence test to evaluate to true. Here, the first publisher is P01 (Abatis Publishers). The DBMS ascertains whether any rows exist in the table *titles* in which *pub_id* is P01 and *type* is biography. If so, Abatis Publishers is included in the final result. The DBMS repeats the same process for each of the other publisher IDs. To list the names of publishers that *haven't* published biographies, change EXISTS to NOT EXISTS.

```
SELECT pub_name
  FROM publishers p
  WHERE EXISTS
    (SELECT *
       FROM titles t
       WHERE t.pub_id = p.pub_id AND type = 'biography');
```

The result is:

```
pub_name
-------------------
Abatis Publishers
Schadenfreude Press
```

You can use EXISTS to find an **intersection** (that is, retrieve the rows that two tables have in common). The following query lists the cities in which both an author and publisher are located. To find a **difference** (that is, retrieve the rows in one table that aren't also in another table), change EXISTS to NOT EXISTS.

```
SELECT DISTINCT city
  FROM authors a
  WHERE EXISTS
    (SELECT * FROM publishers p WHERE p.city = a.city);
```

The result is:

```
city
-------------
New York
San Francisco
```

The following query lists the authors who wrote (or cowrote) three or more books.

```
SELECT au_id, au_fname, au_lname
  FROM authors a
  WHERE EXISTS
    (SELECT *
       FROM title_authors ta
       WHERE ta.au_id = a.au_id
       HAVING COUNT(*) >= 3);
```

The result is:

```
au_id au_fname au_lname
----- -------- ---------
A01   Sarah    Buchman
A02   Wendy    Heydemark
A04   Klee     Hull
A06            Kellsey
```

DBMS To run the preceding query in **Microsoft Access**, **PostgreSQL**, and **DB2**, change `SELECT *` to `SELECT 1`.

The following query uses two existence tests to list the authors who wrote (or cowrote) both children's and psychology books.

```
SELECT au_id, au_fname, au_lname
  FROM authors a
  WHERE EXISTS
    (SELECT *
       FROM title_authors ta
       INNER JOIN titles t ON t.title_id = ta.title_id
       WHERE ta.au_id = a.au_id AND t.type = 'children')
  AND EXISTS
    (SELECT *
       FROM title_authors ta
       INNER JOIN titles t ON t.title_id = ta.title_id
       WHERE ta.au_id = a.au_id AND t.type = 'psychology');
```

The result is:

```
au_id au_fname au_lname
----- -------- --------
A06            Kellsey
```

The following query performs a uniqueness test to determine whether duplicates occur in the column *au_id* in the table *title_authors*. The query prints *Yes* if duplicate values exist in the column *au_id*; otherwise, it returns an empty result. You can add grouping columns to the GROUP BY clause to determine whether multiple-column duplicates exist.

```
SELECT DISTINCT 'Yes' AS "Duplicates?"
  WHERE EXISTS
    (SELECT *
       FROM title_authors
       GROUP BY au_id
       HAVING COUNT(*) > 1);
```

The result is:

```
Duplicates?
-----------
Yes
```

DBMS To run the preceding query in **Microsoft Access**, **PostgreSQL**, and **DB2**, change `SELECT *` to `SELECT 1`. Also, in **Microsoft Access** and **MySQL**, add the clause `FROM title_authors` to the outer query. To run it in **Oracle**, add the clause `FROM DUAL` to the outer query. To run it in **DB2**, add the clause `FROM SYSIBM.SYSDUMMY1` to the outer query. (For Oracle and DB2, see the DBMS tip in "Tips for derived columns" on page 65.)

CHAPTER 18

Combining Queries

Combining Rows with UNION

The UNION operator combines the results of two queries into a single result that has the rows returned by both queries, optionally removing duplicate rows from the result. The syntax of a UNION statement is:

```
select_query1
UNION [ALL]
select_query2;
```

- Duplicate rows are eliminated from the result unless ALL is specified.
- The SELECT-clause lists in the two queries must have the same number of columns (column names, arithmetic expressions, aggregate functions, and so on).
- The corresponding columns in the two queries must be listed in the same order in the two queries.
- The corresponding columns must have the same data type or must be implicitly convertible to the same type (page 77).
- If the names of corresponding columns match, that column name is used in the result. If the corresponding column names differ, it's up to the DBMS to determine the column name in the result. Most DBMSs take the result's column names from the first SELECT query in the union. If you want to rename a column in the result, use an AS clause (page 28) in the first query.

- An ORDER BY clause (Chapter 5) can appear in only the final SELECT query in the union. The sort is applied to the final, combined result. Because the result's column names depend on the DBMS, it's often easiest to use relative column positions to specify the sort order.
- GROUP BY and HAVING (Chapter 14) can be specified in the individual queries only; they can't be used to affect the final result.

Tip: Note that a union, which stacks rows atop one another, differs from a join, which combines columns from two tables.

The following query lists the states where authors and publishers are located. By default, UNION removes duplicate rows from the result.

```
SELECT state FROM authors
UNION
SELECT state FROM publishers;
```

The result is:

```
state
-----
NULL
CA
CO
FL
NY
```

If you change UNION to UNION ALL in the preceding query, then all rows are included in the result (that is, duplicates aren't removed):

```
state
-----
NY
CO
CA
CA
NY
CA
FL
NY
CA
NULL
CA
```

The following query lists the names of all the authors and publishers located in New York state and the titles of books published in New York state, sorted by type and then by name. The AS clauses in the first query name the columns in the result. The derived column *Type* identifies which table each row came from. The WHERE conditions retrieve the authors and publishers from New York state only. The ORDER BY clause uses relative column positions instead of column names to sort the result.

```
SELECT
    'author' AS "Type",
    au_fname || ' ' || au_lname AS "Name"
  FROM authors
  WHERE state = 'NY'
UNION
SELECT
    'publisher',
    pub_name
  FROM publishers
  WHERE state = 'NY'
UNION
SELECT
    'title',
    title_name
  FROM titles t
  INNER JOIN publishers p
    ON t.pub_id = p.pub_id
  WHERE p.state = 'NY'
  ORDER BY 1 ASC, 2 ASC;
```

The result is:

```
Type      Name
--------- --------------------------
author    Christian Kells
author    Sarah Buchman
publisher Abatis Publishers
title     1977!
title     How About Never?
title     Not Without My Faberge Egg
title     Spontaneous, Not Annoying
```

DBMS To run the preceding query in **Microsoft Access** and **Microsoft SQL Server**, change the concatenation expression (page 71) to `au_fname + ' ' + au_lname`. In **MySQL**, change the concatenation expression to `CONCAT(au_fname, ' ', au_lname)`.

The following query is similar to the preceding one except that it lists the counts of each author, publisher, and book, instead of their names.

```
SELECT
    'author' AS "Type",
    COUNT(au_id) AS "Count"
  FROM authors
  WHERE state = 'NY'
UNION
SELECT 'publisher', COUNT(pub_id)
  FROM publishers
  WHERE state = 'NY'
UNION
SELECT 'title', COUNT(title_id)
  FROM titles t
  INNER JOIN publishers p
    ON t.pub_id = p.pub_id
  WHERE p.state = 'NY'
  ORDER BY 1 ASC;
```

The result is:

```
Type      Count
--------- -----
author        2
publisher     1
title         4
```

UNION Commutativity

UNION is commutative: A UNION B is the same as B UNION A. In theory, the order in which the SELECT queries (tables) occur in a union should make no speed difference. But in practice your DBMS might run

```
small_table1 UNION small_table2 UNION big_table;
```

faster than

```
small_table1 UNION big_table UNION small_table2;
```

because of the way the optimizer merges intermediate results and removes duplicate rows. The results are DBMS dependent. Experiment.

The following query raises the price of history books by 10 percent and psychology books by 20 percent, and leaves the prices of other books unchanged. This query is equivalent to the simple CASE query in Chapter 12, but uses multiple UNION queries instead of using CASE to simulate if-then logic.

```
SELECT title_id, type, price,
    price * 1.10 AS "New price"
  FROM titles
  WHERE type = 'history'
UNION
SELECT title_id, type, price, price * 1.20
  FROM titles
  WHERE type = 'psychology'
UNION
SELECT title_id, type, price, price
  FROM titles
  WHERE type NOT IN ('psychology','history')
  ORDER BY type ASC, title_id ASC;
```

The result is:

```
title_id type       price   New price
-------- ---------- ------- ---------
T06      biography    19.95     19.95
T07      biography    23.95     23.95
T10      biography     NULL      NULL
T12      biography    12.99     12.99
T08      children     10.00     10.00
T09      children     13.95     13.95
T03      computer     39.95     39.95
T01      history      21.99     24.19
T02      history      19.95     21.95
T13      history      29.99     32.99
T04      psychology   12.99     15.59
T05      psychology    6.95      8.34
T11      psychology    7.99      9.59
```

Tips for UNION

- Don't use UNION where a compound condition will suffice:

  ```
  SELECT DISTINCT * FROM mytable
    WHERE col1 = 1 AND col2 = 2;
  ```

  usually is faster than

  ```
  SELECT * FROM mytable
    WHERE col1 = 1;
  UNION
  SELECT * FROM mytable
    WHERE col2 = 2;
  ```

- If you mix UNION and UNION ALL in a single statement, use parentheses to specify order of evaluation. Take these two statements, for example:

  ```
  SELECT * FROM table1
  UNION ALL
  (SELECT * FROM table2
  UNION
  SELECT * FROM table3);
  ```

  and:

  ```
  (SELECT * FROM table1
  UNION ALL
  SELECT * FROM table2)
  UNION
  SELECT * FROM table3;
  ```

  The first statement eliminates duplicates in the union of *table2* and *table3* but doesn't eliminate duplicates in the union of that result and *table1*. The second statement includes duplicates in the union of *table1* and *table2* but eliminates duplicates in the subsequent union with *table3*, so ALL has no effect on the final result of this statement.

- For UNION operations, the DBMS performs an internal sort to identify and remove duplicate rows; hence, the result of a UNION might be sorted even if you don't specify an ORDER BY clause. UNION ALL doesn't sort because it doesn't need to remove duplicates. Sorting is computationally expensive—don't use UNION when UNION ALL will suffice.

CHAPTER 19

Inserting Rows

Modifying Table Data

To this point, you've used the SELECT statement to retrieve and analyze the data in tables, but you can also use SQL to *modify* table data:

- The INSERT statement adds new rows to a table (this chapter).
- The UPDATE statement changes the values in a table's existing rows (Chapter 20).
- The DELETE statement removes rows from a table (Chapter 20).

These statements don't return a result, but your DBMS normally will print a message indicating whether the statement ran successfully and, if so, the number of rows affected by the change. To see the actual effect the statement had on a table, use a SELECT statement.

Unlike SELECT, which only accesses data, these statements change data, so your database administrator might need to grant you permission to run them.

The process of adding rows to a table for the first time is called **populating the table**.

Displaying Table Definitions

To use INSERT, UPDATE, or DELETE, you must know about the columns of the table whose data you're modifying, including:

- The order of the columns in the table
- Each column's name

- Each column's data type
- Whether a column is a key (or part of a key)
- Whether a column's values must be unique within that column
- Whether a column allows nulls
- Each column's default value (if any)
- Table and column constraints (Chapter 21)

Table definitions of the sample-database tables are given in Appendix A, but you can get the same information by using DBMS tools that describe database objects. This section explains how to use those tools to display table definitions for the current database.

To display table definitions in Microsoft Access:

- In Access 2007 or later, press F11 to show the Navigation pane (on the left), and then right-click the table name and choose Design View from the shortcut menu. (If tables aren't visible in the Navigation pane, click the menu at the top of the pane and choose Object Type, and then click the menu again and choose Tables.)

  or

  In Access 2003 or earlier, press F11 to show the Database window, click Tables (below Objects), click a table in the list, and then click Design in the toolbar to open the table in Design View.

To display table definitions in Microsoft SQL Server:

1 Start SQL Server Management Studio or the interactive sqlcmd command-line tool (page 222).

  The sqlcmd command display a few pages that speed by. It's easier to use the graphical tools and choose Query > Results to Grid (or Results in Grid).

2 Type `sp_help` *`table`*.

  table is a table name.

3 In SQL Server Management Studio, choose Query > Execute or press F5.

  or

  In sqlcmd, press Enter, and then type go and press Enter.

To display table definitions in Oracle:

1. Start the interactive sqlplus command-line tool (page 224).
2. Type `describe table;` and then press Enter.

   table is a table name.

To display table definitions in IBM DB2:

1. Start Command Center or the db2 command-line processor (page 226).
2. Type `describe table table;` and then press Enter (or Ctrl+Enter in Command Center).

   table is a table name.

To display table definitions in MySQL:

1. Start the interactive mysql command-line tool (page 230).
2. Type `describe table;` and then press Enter.

   table is a table name.

To display table definitions in PostgreSQL:

1. Start the interactive psql command-line tool (page 232).
2. Type `\d table` and then press Enter.

   table is a table name. Note that you don't terminate this command with a semicolon.

DBMS Table 19.1 shows the commands and queries that list the tables in the current database.

Table 19.1 Listing Database Tables

DBMS	Command or Query
Access	Navigation pane (press F11)
SQL Server	sp_tables
Oracle	SELECT * FROM TAB;
DB2	LIST TABLES;
MySQL	SHOW TABLES;
PostgreSQL	\d

Inserting Rows with INSERT

The INSERT statement adds new rows to a table. This section explains how to use several variations of INSERT to:

- Insert a row by using column positions (INSERT VALUES)
- Insert a row by using column names (INSERT VALUES)
- Insert rows from one table into another table (INSERT SELECT)

The important characteristics of INSERT are:

- In a positional insert, you insert ordered values into a new row in the same sequence as the columns appear in a table. In a named-column insert, you name the specific column into which each value is inserted in the new row.

  You always should use a named-column insert so your SQL code still will work if someone reorders the table's columns or adds new columns.
- With INSERT VALUES, you specify explicit values to insert into a table. With INSERT SELECT, you choose rows from another table to insert into a table.
- INSERT VALUES adds one row to a table. INSERT SELECT adds zero or more rows to a table.
- Each inserted value must have the same data type or must be implicitly convertible to the same type as its corresponding column (see "Converting Data Types" on page 77).
- To preserve referential integrity, an inserted foreign-key value must contain either null (if allowed) or an existing key value from the primary or unique key column referenced by the foreign key (see "Foreign Keys" on page 13).
- An inserted value can't violate a check constraint (page 183).
- No expression can cause an arithmetic error (an overflow or divide-by-zero error, for example).
- Recall from "Tables" on page 8 that the order of rows in a table is unimportant and that you have no control over the physical location of rows, so new rows can appear anywhere among a table's existing rows.

Tip: If you're using transactions (Chapter 24), you must use a COMMIT statement after your final INSERT statement to make the changes to the table permanent.

Inserting a row by using column positions

To insert a row by using column positions, type:

```
INSERT INTO table
  VALUES(value1, value2,..., valueN);
```

table is the name of a table to insert the row into. *value1, value2,..., valueN* is a parenthesized list of comma-separated literals or expressions that provides a value to every column in the new row.

The number of values must equal the number of columns in *table*, and the values must be listed in the same sequence as the columns in *table*. The DBMS inserts each value into the column that corresponds to the value's position in *table*. *value1* is inserted into the first column of *table* in the new row, *value2* into the second column, and so on.

The following INSERT statement adds a new row to the table *authors* by listing values in the same order in which columns are defined in *authors*.

```
INSERT INTO authors
  VALUES(
    'A08',
    'Michael',
    'Polk',
    '512-953-1231',
    '4028 Guadalupe St',
    'Austin',
    'TX',
    '78701');
```

Tip: Check the DBMS documentation to see how your DBMS handles updating values in columns whose data type generates a unique row identifier automatically (see "Unique Identifiers" on page 254).

Inserting a row by using column names

To insert a row by using column names, type:

```
INSERT INTO table(column1, column2,..., columnN)
  VALUES(value1, value2,..., valueN);
```

table is the name of the table to insert the row into. *column1*, *column2*,..., *columnN* is a parenthesized list of comma-separated names of columns in *table*. *value1*, *value2*,..., *valueN* is a parenthesized list of comma-separated literals or expressions that provides values to the named columns in the new row.

The number of values must equal the number of columns in the column list, and the values must be listed in the same sequence as the column names. The DBMS inserts each value into a column by using corresponding list positions. *value1* is inserted into *column1* in the new row, *value2* into *column2*, and so on. An omitted column is assigned its default value or null.

It's clearer to list column names in the same order as they appear in the table, but you can list them in any order. In either case, the values in the VALUES clause must match the sequence in which you list the column names.

The following INSERT statement adds a new row to the table *authors* by listing column names and values in the same order in which columns are defined in *authors*.

```
INSERT INTO authors(
    au_id,
    au_fname,
    au_lname,
    phone,
    address,
    city,
    state,
    zip)
  VALUES(
    'A09',
    'Irene',
    'Bell',
    '415-225-4689',
    '810 Throckmorton Ave',
    'Mill Valley',
    'CA',
    '94941');
```

You don't have to list column names in the same order in which they're defined in the table. The following INSERT statement rearranges the column names and their corresponding values.

```
INSERT INTO authors(
    zip,
    phone,
    address,
    au_lname,
    au_fname,
    state,
    au_id,
    city)
  VALUES(
    '60614',
    '312-998-0020',
    '1937 N. Clark St',
    'Weston',
    'Dianne',
    'IL',
    'A10',
    'Chicago');
```

You can omit column names if you want to provide values for only some columns explicitly. If you omit a column, the DBMS must be able to provide a value based on the column's definition. The DBMS will insert the column's default value (if defined) or null (if allowed). If you omit a column that doesn't have a default value or allow nulls, the DBMS will display an error message and won't insert the row.

The following INSERT statement adds a row for a new author but omits column names and values for the author's address information. The DBMS inserts nulls into the omitted columns automatically. In this case, the VALUES clause is equivalent to VALUES('A11', 'Max', 'Allard', '212-502-0955', NULL, NULL, NULL, NULL). For information about specifying a default value and allowing nulls, see Chapter 21.

```
INSERT INTO authors(au_id, au_fname, au_lname, phone)
  VALUES('A11', 'Max', 'Allard', '212-502-0955');
```

Insert rows from one table into another table

To insert rows from one table into another table, type:

```
INSERT INTO table[(column1, column2,..., columnN)]
  subquery;
```

table is the name of table to insert the rows into. *column1*, *column2*,..., *columnN* is an optional parenthesized list of comma-separated names of columns in *table*. *subquery* is a SELECT query that returns rows to insert into *table*.

The number of columns in the *subquery* result must equal the number of columns in *table* or in the column list. The DBMS ignores the column names in the *subquery* result and uses column position instead. The first column in the *subquery* result is used to populate the first column in *table* or *column1*, and so on. An omitted column is assigned its default value or null.

The following examples use the hypothetical table *new_publishers*, which has the same structure as the table *publishers* and acts as the source of new rows.

The following INSERT statement inserts the rows for Los Angeles-based publishers from *new_publishers* into *publishers*. Here, the column list is omitted, so the DBMS uses the column positions in *publishers* rather than column names to insert values.

```
INSERT INTO publishers
  SELECT
      pub_id,
      pub_name,
      city,
      state,
      country
    FROM new_publishers
    WHERE city = 'Los Angeles';
```

The following INSERT statement inserts the rows for non-U.S. publishers from *new_publishers* into *publishers*. Here, the column names are the same in both the INSERT and SELECT clauses, but they don't have to match because the DBMS disregards the names of the columns returned by SELECT and uses their positions instead.

```
INSERT INTO publishers(
    pub_id,
    pub_name,
    city,
    state,
    country)
  SELECT
      pub_id,
      pub_name,
      city,
      state,
      country
    FROM new_publishers
    WHERE country <> 'USA';
```

It's legal for the SELECT query to return an empty result (zero rows). The following INSERT statement inserts the rows for publishers named XXX from *new_publishers* into *publishers*. I can use SELECT * instead of listing column names because *new_publishers* and *publishers* have the same structure. This statement inserts no rows into *publishers* because no publisher is named XXX in *new_publishers*.

```
INSERT INTO publishers(
    pub_id,
    pub_name,
    city,
    state,
    country)
  SELECT *
    FROM new_publishers
    WHERE pub_name = 'XXX';
```

Tip: If *table1* and *table2* have compatible structures, you can insert all the rows from *table2* into *table1* with `INSERT INTO` ***`table1`*** `SELECT * FROM` ***`table2`***`;`.

CHAPTER 20

Updating and Deleting Rows

Updating Rows with UPDATE

The UPDATE statement changes the values in a table's existing rows. You can use UPDATE to change:

- All rows in a table
- Specific rows in a table

To update rows, you specify:

- The table to update
- The names of the columns to update and their new values
- An optional search condition that specifies which rows to update

The important characteristics of UPDATE are:

- UPDATE takes an optional WHERE clause that specifies which rows to update. Without a WHERE clause, UPDATE changes *all* the rows in the table.
- UPDATE is dangerous because it's easy to omit the WHERE clause mistakenly (and update all rows) or misspecify the WHERE search condition (and update the wrong rows). It's wise to run a SELECT statement that uses the same WHERE clause before running the actual UPDATE statement. Use SELECT * to display all rows that the DBMS will change when you run UPDATE, or use SELECT COUNT(*) to display only the number of rows that will change.

- Each updated value must have the same data type or must be implicitly convertible to the same type as its column (see "Converting Data Types" on page 77).
- To preserve referential integrity, you can define the action that the DBMS takes automatically when you try to UPDATE a key value to which foreign-key values point (page 177).
- An updated value can't violate a check constraint (page 183).
- No expression can cause an arithmetic error (an overflow or divide-by-zero error, for example).
- Recall from "Tables" on page 8 that the order of rows in a table is unimportant and that you have no control over the physical location of rows, so an updated row can change position in a table.

To update rows, type:

```
UPDATE table
  SET column = expr
  [WHERE search_condition];
```

table is the name of a table to update.

column is the name of the column in *table* that contains the rows to change. *expr* is a literal, an expression, or a parenthesized subquery that returns a single value. The value returned by *expr* replaces the existing value in *column*. To change the values in multiple columns, type a list of comma-separated *column* = *expr* expressions in the SET clause. You can list the *column* = *expr* expressions in any order.

search_condition specifies the conditions that rows have to meet to be updated. The *search_condition* conditions can be WHERE conditions (comparison operators, LIKE, BETWEEN, IN, or IS NULL) or subquery conditions (comparison operators, IN, ALL, ANY, or EXISTS), combined with AND, OR, or NOT. If the WHERE clause is omitted, every row in *table* is updated.

Tip: If you're using transactions (Chapter 24), you must use a COMMIT statement after your final UPDATE statement to make the changes to the table permanent.

The following UPDATE statement changes the value of *contract* to zero in every row of *titles*. The lack of a WHERE clause tells the DBMS to update all the rows in the column *contract*. This statement updates 13 rows.

```
UPDATE titles
  SET contract = 0;
```

The following UPDATE statement uses an arithmetic expression and a WHERE condition to double the price of history books. This statement updates three rows.

```
UPDATE titles
  SET price = price * 2.0
  WHERE type = 'history';
```

The following UPDATE statement updates the columns *type* and *pages* for psychology books. You use only a single SET clause to update multiple columns, with *column* = *expr* expressions separated by commas. (Don't put a comma after the last expression.) This statement updates three rows.

```
UPDATE titles
  SET type = 'self help',
      pages = NULL
  WHERE type = 'psychology';
```

The following UPDATE statement uses a subquery and an aggregate function to cut the sales of books with above-average sales in half. This statement updates two rows. (This example won't run in **MySQL** because MySQL forbids the same table (*titles*, in this case) from appearing in both the subquery's FROM clause and the update target.)

```
UPDATE titles
  SET sales = sales * 0.5
  WHERE sales > (SELECT AVG(sales) FROM titles);
```

You can update values in a given table based on the values stored in another table. The following UPDATE statement uses nested subqueries to update the publication date for all the books written (or cowritten) by Sarah Buchman. This statement updates three rows.

```
UPDATE titles
  SET pubdate = DATE '2003-01-01'
  WHERE title_id IN
    (SELECT title_id
       FROM title_authors
       WHERE au_id IN
         (SELECT au_id
            FROM authors
            WHERE au_fname = 'Sarah'
              AND au_lname = 'Buchman'));
```

DBMS To run the preceding example in **Microsoft Access** change the date literal to #2003-01-01# (without DATE). In **Microsoft SQL Server** and **DB2**, change the date literal to '2003-01-01' (without DATE).

Suppose that Abatis Publishers (publisher P01) swallows Tenterhooks Press (P04) in a merger, so now, all the Tenterhooks Press books are published by Abatis Publishers. The following UPDATE statement works in a bottom-up fashion to change the publisher IDs in *titles* from P04 to P01. The WHERE subquery retrieves the *pub_id* for Tenterhooks Press. The DBMS uses this *pub_id* to retrieve the books in the table *titles* whose publisher is Tenterhooks Press. Finally, the DBMS uses the value returned by the SET subquery to update the appropriate rows in the table *titles*. Because the subqueries are used with an unmodified comparison operator, they must be scalar subqueries that return a single value (that is, a one-row, one-column result). This statement updates five rows.

```
UPDATE titles
  SET pub_id =
    (SELECT pub_id
       FROM publishers
       WHERE pub_name = 'Abatis Publishers')
  WHERE pub_id =
    (SELECT pub_id
       FROM publishers
       WHERE pub_name = 'Tenterhooks Press');
```

DBMS **Microsoft Access** doesn't support scalar subqueries in the SET clause. To run preceding example, split the UPDATE statement into two statements: one that SELECTs the *pub_id* for Abatis Publishers from *publishers* and one that uses this *pub_id* to change the *pub_id* of all the Tenterhooks Press books in *titles*. Then run the statements programmatically (in a host language such as Visual Basic or C#), using the result of the first statement as the input for the second statement.

Tip: Check the DBMS documentation to see how your DBMS handles updating values in columns whose data type generates a unique row identifier automatically (see "Unique Identifiers" on page 254).

Deleting Rows with DELETE

The DELETE statement removes rows from a table. You can use DELETE to remove:

- All rows in a table
- Specific rows in a table

To delete rows, you specify:

- The table whose rows to delete
- An optional search condition that specifies which rows to delete

The important characteristics of DELETE are:

- Unlike INSERT and UPDATE, DELETE takes no column names because it removes entire rows.
- DELETE removes rows from a table, but it never deletes the table's definition. Even if you remove all rows from a table, the table itself still exists. To delete a table definition, use DROP TABLE (page 188).
- DELETE takes an optional WHERE clause that specifies which rows to delete. Without a WHERE clause, DELETE removes *all* the rows in the table.
- DELETE is dangerous because it's easy to omit the WHERE clause mistakenly (and remove all rows) or misspecify the WHERE search condition (and remove the wrong rows). It's wise to run a SELECT statement that uses the same WHERE clause before running the actual DELETE statement. Use SELECT * to display all rows that the DBMS will remove when you run DELETE, or use SELECT COUNT(*) to display only the number of rows that will disappear.
- To preserve referential integrity, you can define the action the DBMS takes automatically when you try to DELETE a key value to which foreign-key values point (page 177).
- No expression can cause an arithmetic error (an overflow or divide-by-zero error, for example).
- Recall from "Tables" on page 8 that the order of rows in a table is unimportant and that you have no control over the physical location of rows, so a deletion might reorder the positions of the rows remaining in a table.

To delete rows, type:

```
DELETE FROM table
  [WHERE search_condition];
```

table is the name of a table to delete rows from.

search_condition specifies the conditions to be met for the rows that are deleted. The *search_condition* conditions can be WHERE conditions (comparison operators, LIKE, BETWEEN, IN, or IS NULL) or subquery conditions (comparison operators, IN, ALL, ANY, or EXISTS), combined with AND, OR, or NOT. If the WHERE clause is omitted, every row in *table* is deleted.

Tip: If you're using transactions (Chapter 24), you must use a COMMIT statement after your final DELETE statement to make the changes to the table permanent.

Note that the following examples ignore referential-integrity constraints—which you wouldn't do in a production database, of course.

The following DELETE statement deletes every row in *royalties*. The lack of a WHERE clause tells the DBMS to delete all the rows. This statement deletes 13 rows.

```
DELETE FROM royalties;
```

The WHERE clause in the following DELETE statement tells the DBMS to remove the authors with the last name Hull from *authors*. This statement deletes two rows.

```
DELETE FROM authors
  WHERE au_lname = 'Hull';
```

You can delete rows in a given table based on the values stored in another table. The following DELETE statement uses a subquery to remove all the books published by publishers P01 or P04 from *title_authors*. This statement deletes 12 rows.

```
DELETE FROM title_authors
  WHERE title_id IN
    (SELECT title_id
       FROM titles
       WHERE pub_id IN ('P01', 'P04'));
```

CHAPTER 21

Creating and Changing Tables

The TABLE Statements

Many DBMSs have interactive, graphical tools that let you create and manage tables and table properties such as column definitions and constraints. This chapter explains how to perform those tasks programmatically by using SQL:

- The CREATE TABLE statement creates a new table.
- The ALTER TABLE statement modifies the structure of an existing table.
- The DROP TABLE statement destroys a table and all its data.

These statements don't return a result, but your DBMS might print a message indicating whether the statement ran successfully. To see the actual effect the statement had on a table, examine the table's structure by using one of the commands described in "Displaying Table Definitions" on page 151.

These statements modify database objects and data, so your database administrator might need to grant you permission to run them.

Creating Tables

Recall from Chapter 2 that a database is organized around tables. To a user or an SQL programmer, a database appears to be a collection of one or more tables (and nothing but tables). To create a table, you specify the following:

- Table name
- Column names
- Data types of the columns
- Default values of columns
- Constraints

The table name and the column names must conform to the rules for SQL identifiers (page 20). The data type (Appendix C) of each column is a character, numeric, datetime, or other data type. A **default** is the value the column takes if you don't specify a value explicitly. **Constraints** define properties such as nullability, keys, and permissible values.

You create a new table by using the CREATE TABLE statement, whose general syntax is:

```
CREATE TABLE table
  (
  column1 data_type1 [col_constraints1],
  column2 data_type2 [col_constraints2],
  ...
  columnN data_typeN [col_constraintsN]
  [, table_constraint1]
  [, table_constraint2]
  ...
  [, table_constraintM]
  );
```

Each column definition has a column name, a data type, and an optional list of one or more column constraints. An optional list of table constraints follows the final column definition.

Understanding Constraints

Constraints let you define rules for values allowed in columns (Table 21.1). Your DBMS uses these rules to enforce the integrity of information in the database automatically.

Constraints come in two flavors:

- A **column constraint** is part of a column definition and imposes a condition on that column only.
- A **table constraint** is declared independently of a column definition and can impose a condition on more than one column in a table. You must use a table constraint to include more than one column in a single constraint.

You can specify some constraints as either column or table constraints, depending on the context in which they're used. If a primary key contains one column, for example, you can define it as either a column constraint or a table constraint. If the primary key has two or more columns, you must use a table constraint.

Assigning names to constraints lets you manage them efficiently; you can change or delete a named constraint by using the ALTER TABLE statement, for example. Constraint names are optional, but many SQL programmers and database designers name *all* constraints. It's not uncommon to leave a NOT NULL constraint unnamed, but you always should name other types of constraints (even if that's not the case in some of the following examples).

Table 21.1 Constraints

Constraint	Description
NOT NULL	Prevents nulls from being inserted into a column
PRIMARY KEY	Sets the table's primary-key column(s)
FOREIGN KEY	Sets the table's foreign-key column(s)
UNIQUE	Prevents duplicate values from being inserted into a column
CHECK	Limits the values that can be inserted into a column by using logical (Boolean) expressions

If you don't name a constraint explicitly, your DBMS will generate a name and assign it to the constraint quietly and automatically. System-assigned names often contain strings of random characters and are cumbersome to use, so use the CONSTRAINT clause to assign your own name instead. Constraint names also appear in warnings, error messages, and logs, which is another good reason to name constraints yourself.

To name a constraint, preceding a constraint definition, type:

```
CONSTRAINT constraint_name
```

constraint_name is the name of the constraint and is a valid SQL identifier (page 20). Constraints names must be unique within a table.

Creating a New Table with CREATE TABLE

This section describes how to create a new table by using a minimal CREATE TABLE statement. Subsequent sections show you how to add column and table constraints to CREATE TABLE.

To create a new table, type:

```
CREATE TABLE table
  (
  column1 data_type1,
  column2 data_type2,
  ...
  columnN data_typeN
  );
```

table is the name of the new table to create.

column1, column2,..., columnN are the names of the columns in *table*. You must create at least one column.

data_type1, data_type2,..., data_typeN specify the SQL data type (Appendix C) of each corresponding column. A data type can specify a length, scale, or precision, where applicable.

The table name must be unique within the database, and each column name must be unique within the table.

Tip: To see the result of a CREATE TABLE statement, examine the table's structure by using one of the commands described in "Displaying Table Definitions" on page 151.

The following CREATE TABLE statement creates the sample-database table *titles*.

```
CREATE TABLE titles
  (
  title_id   CHAR(3)      ,
  title_name VARCHAR(40)  ,
  type       VARCHAR(10)  ,
  pub_id     CHAR(3)      ,
  pages      INTEGER      ,
  price      DECIMAL(5,2),
  sales      INTEGER      ,
  pubdate    DATE         ,
  contract   SMALLINT
  );
```

DBMS To run the preceding example in **Microsoft SQL Server**, change the data type of the column *pubdate* to DATETIME.

Forbidding Nulls with NOT NULL

A column's nullability determines whether its rows can contain nulls—that is, whether values are required or optional in the column. A null represents a missing, unknown, or inapplicable value. A null in the column *price* doesn't mean that an item has no price or that its price is zero; it means that the price is unknown or has not been set. For details, see "Nulls" on page 22.

Tip: Nulls belong to no data type and can be inserted into any column that allows nulls.

When you're defining a nullability constraint, some important considerations are:

- A nullability constraint always is a column constraint and not a table constraint (page 169).
- You define a nullability constraint by using the keywords NOT NULL in a CREATE TABLE column definition.
- In general, avoid allowing nulls because they complicate queries, insertions, and updates.
- Forbidding nulls in a column can help maintain data integrity by ensuring that users entering data must enter a value in the column. The DBMS won't insert or update a row if a non-nullable column contains a null.

- Some other constraints, such as a PRIMARY KEY constraint, can't be used with nullable columns.
- Nulls affect referential-integrity checks in foreign keys (page 177).
- If you INSERT a row (Chapter 19) but include no value for a column that allows null values, your DBMS supplies a null (unless a DEFAULT clause exists).
- If you don't specify a NOT NULL constraint, the column accepts nulls by default.

The following CREATE TABLE statement creates the sample-database table *titles*, forbidding nulls in some columns.

```
CREATE TABLE titles
  (
  title_id   CHAR(3)      NOT NULL,
  title_name VARCHAR(40)  NOT NULL,
  type       VARCHAR(10)          ,
  pub_id     CHAR(3)      NOT NULL,
  pages      INTEGER              ,
  price      DECIMAL(5,2)         ,
  sales      INTEGER              ,
  pubdate    DATE                 ,
  contract   SMALLINT     NOT NULL
  );
```

DBMS To run the preceding example in **Microsoft SQL Server**, change the data type of the column *pubdate* to DATETIME. **Oracle** treats an empty string ('') as a null (see the DBMS tip in "Tips for nulls" on page 23). For **all DBMSs**, check the documentation to see how your DBMS handles nullability constraints for columns whose data type generates a unique row identifier automatically (see "Unique Identifiers" on page 254).

Specifying a Default Value with DEFAULT

A **default** specifies a value that your DBMS assigns to a column if you omit a value for the column when inserting a row (Chapter 19). When you're defining a default value, some important considerations are:

- A default applies to a single column.
- You define a default by using the keyword DEFAULT in a CREATE TABLE column definition.

- The default must have the same data type or must be implicitly convertible to the same type as its column (see "Converting Data Types" on page 77).
- The column must be long enough to hold the default value.
- If you INSERT a row without specifying a value for a column, that column's default is used. If the column definition has no DEFAULT, the default is null.
- If a column has no DEFAULT and is declared NOT NULL, you should specify the column's value explicitly when you INSERT a row. If you omit an explicit value in this situation, some DBMSs will refuse to INSERT the row, whereas others will assign a default automatically based on the column's date type. **MySQL**, for example, assigns a default value of zero to numeric, non-nullable columns without explicit defaults.

To define a column's default value, add the clause

```
DEFAULT expr
```

to a CREATE TABLE column definition. *expr* is an expression that evaluates to a constant, such as a literal, a built-in function, a mathematical expression, or NULL. If no default is specified, NULL is assumed.

The following CREATE TABLE statement assigns defaults to some of the columns in the sample-database table *titles*. The columns *title_id* and *pub_id* are NOT NULL and have no default values, so you must provide explicit values for them in an INSERT statement. The *pages* clause DEFAULT NULL is equivalent to omitting the DEFAULT. The *pubdate* and *contract* defaults show that the defaults can be expressions more complex than plain literals.

```
CREATE TABLE titles
  (
  title_id   CHAR(3)      NOT NULL                          ,
  title_name VARCHAR(40)  NOT NULL DEFAULT ''               ,
  type       VARCHAR(10)           DEFAULT 'undefined'      ,
  pub_id     CHAR(3)      NOT NULL                          ,
  pages      INTEGER               DEFAULT NULL             ,
  price      DECIMAL(5,2) NOT NULL DEFAULT 0.00             ,
  sales      INTEGER                                        ,
  pubdate    DATE                  DEFAULT CURRENT_DATE,
  contract   SMALLINT     NOT NULL DEFAULT (3*7)-21
  );
```

DBMSs and Default Values

DBMS DBMSs vary a bit in what they will and will not accept as default values. To run the preceding CREATE TABLE example, you must modify the defaults in the following DBMSs.

Microsoft Access doesn't allow arithmetic expressions in a DEFAULT clause; use a numeric literal. Use Date() instead of CURRENT_DATE to return the system date (page 76). To run the preceding example, change the default clause of the column *pubdate* to DEFAULT Date() and the default clause of the column *contract* to DEFAULT 0.

Microsoft SQL Server doesn't support the data type DATE; use DATETIME instead. Use GETDATE() instead of CURRENT_DATE to return the system date (page 76). To run the preceding example, change the *pubdate* column's data type to DATETIME, and change its default clause to DEFAULT GETDATE().

In **Oracle**, the DEFAULT clause follows the data type and precedes all column constraints, including the nullability constraint. To run the preceding example, swap all the NOT NULL and DEFAULT expressions. For example, change

```
price    DECIMAL(5,2)    NOT NULL          DEFAULT 0.00,
```

to

```
price    DECIMAL(5,2)    DEFAULT 0.00      NOT NULL,
```

Oracle 9i and later versions support CURRENT_DATE (page 76). In Oracle 8i and earlier, use SYSDATE instead of CURRENT_DATE. Oracle treats an empty string ('') as null, so change the *title_name* default to a space character (' ').

DB2 doesn't support arithmetic expressions as default values. To run the preceding example, change the default clause of the column *contract* to DEFAULT 0.

In **MySQL**, a default value must be a literal and not a function or expression. This restriction means that you can't set the default of a date column to CURRENT_DATE. To run the preceding example, delete the DEFAULT clause of the column *pubdate* (or change the default expression to a datetime literal), and change the DEFAULT clause of the column *contract* to DEFAULT 0. (Exception: You can specify CURRENT_TIMESTAMP as the default for a TIMESTAMP column.)

Specifying a Primary Key with PRIMARY KEY

A primary key (page 11) identifies each row uniquely in a table, so no two rows can have the same primary-key value (primary keys don't allow nulls). Each table has exactly one primary key. A one-column key is a simple key; a multiple-column key is a composite key. In a composite key, values can be duplicated within one column, but each combination of values from all the key's columns must be unique.

When you're defining a primary-key constraint, some important considerations are:

- A simple key can be a column constraint or a table constraint; a composite key always is a table constraint (page 169).
- You define a primary-key constraint by using the keywords PRIMARY KEY in a CREATE TABLE definition.
- As a table constraint, PRIMARY KEY makes you specify column name(s) explicitly. As a column constraint, PRIMARY KEY applies to the column in which it's defined.
- The SQL standard lets you create a table without a primary key. In practice, you always should define a primary key for every table.
- No more than one primary-key constraint is allowed in a table.
- In practice, primary-key constraints almost always are named explicitly. To name a constraint, use a CONSTRAINT clause (page 169).
- The nullability of all PRIMARY KEY columns must be NOT NULL (page 171). If you don't specify a nullability constraint, the DBMS sets all primary-key columns to NOT NULL implicitly.
- You must specify a primary-key value explicitly when you INSERT a row (Chapter 19) unless the column's data type generates a unique row identifier automatically (page 254).
- Primary-key values normally don't change after they're inserted.
- For considerations related to inserting, updating, and deleting primary keys that are referenced by foreign keys, see "Specifying a Foreign Key with FOREIGN KEY" on page 177.
- The DBMS will create a unique index (Chapter 22) for a primary key automatically.

The following three CREATE TABLE statements show three equivalent ways to define a simple primary key for the sample-database table *publishers*.

The following example uses a column constraint to designate the primary-key column. This syntax shows the easiest way to create a simple primary key. (In **DB2**, you must add NOT NULL to *pub_id*'s column constraint.)

```
CREATE TABLE publishers
  (
  pub_id    CHAR(3)      PRIMARY KEY,
  pub_name  VARCHAR(20)  NOT NULL    ,
  city      VARCHAR(15)  NOT NULL    ,
  state     CHAR(2)                  ,
  country   VARCHAR(15)  NOT NULL
  );
```

The following example uses an unnamed table constraint to specify the primary key. The explicit NOT NULL column constraint for *pub_id* isn't necessary because the DBMS sets this constraint implicitly and silently.

```
CREATE TABLE publishers
  (
  pub_id    CHAR(3)      NOT NULL,
  pub_name  VARCHAR(20)  NOT NULL,
  city      VARCHAR(15)  NOT NULL,
  state     CHAR(2)              ,
  country   VARCHAR(15)  NOT NULL,
  PRIMARY KEY (pub_id)
  );
```

The following example uses a named table constraint to specify the primary key. This syntax shows the preferred way to add a primary key; you can use the name *publishers_pk* if you decide to change or delete the key later (page 186).

```
CREATE TABLE publishers
  (
  pub_id    CHAR(3)      NOT NULL,
  pub_name  VARCHAR(20)  NOT NULL,
  city      VARCHAR(15)  NOT NULL,
  state     CHAR(2)              ,
  country   VARCHAR(15)  NOT NULL,
  CONSTRAINT publishers_pk
    PRIMARY KEY (pub_id)
  );
```

The following example defines a composite primary key for the sample-database table *title_authors*. The primary-key columns are *title_id* and *au_id*, and the key is named *title_authors_pk*.

```
CREATE TABLE title_authors
  (
  title_id      CHAR(3)      NOT NULL,
  au_id         CHAR(3)      NOT NULL,
  au_order      SMALLINT     NOT NULL,
  royalty_share DECIMAL(5,2) NOT NULL,
  CONSTRAINT title_authors_pk
    PRIMARY KEY (title_id, au_id)
  );
```

Specifying a Foreign Key with FOREIGN KEY

Foreign keys are covered in "Foreign Keys" on page 13. The basics are:

- A foreign key is a mechanism that associates two tables.
- A foreign key is a column (or set of columns) in a table whose values relate to, or reference, values in some other table.
- A foreign key ensures that rows in one table have corresponding rows in another table, called the **referenced table** or **parent table**.
- A foreign key establishes a direct relationship to a primary key or candidate key in the referenced table, so foreign-key values are restricted to parent-key values that already exist. This restriction is called **referential integrity**.
- A foreign key, unlike a primary key, can allow nulls.
- A table can have zero or more foreign keys.
- Foreign-key values generally aren't unique in their own table.
- Foreign-key columns in different tables can reference the same column in a parent table.
- A one-column key is a simple key; a multiple-column key is a composite key.

When you're defining a foreign-key constraint, some important considerations are:

- A simple key can be a column constraint or a table constraint; a composite key always is a table constraint (page 169).

- You define a foreign-key constraint by using the keywords FOREIGN KEY or REFERENCES in a CREATE TABLE definition.
- A foreign key and its parent key can have different column names.
- The foreign key's data type must have the same data type or must be convertible implicitly to the same type as its parent key (see "Converting Data Types" on page 77).
- A FOREIGN KEY column doesn't have to reference only a PRIMARY KEY column in another table; it also can reference a UNIQUE column (page 181) in another table.
- A table can have any number of foreign-key constraints (or none at all).
- In practice, foreign-key constraints almost always are named explicitly. To name a constraint, use a CONSTRAINT clause (page 169).

To specify a simple foreign key as a column constraint, add the following column constraint to a CREATE TABLE column definition:

```
[CONSTRAINT constraint_name]
  REFERENCES ref_table(ref_column)
```

To specify a foreign key as a table constraint, add the following table constraint to a CREATE TABLE definition:

```
[CONSTRAINT constraint_name]
  FOREIGN KEY (key_column)
  REFERENCES ref_table(ref_column)
```

key_column is the name of the foreign-key column. *ref_table* is the name of the parent table referenced by the FOREIGN KEY constraint. *ref_column* is the name of the column in *ref_table* that is the referenced key. For a composite foreign key, specify a list of comma-separated column names in *key_column* and *ref_column* in the table constraint.

The following example uses a column constraint to designate a foreign-key column in the table *titles*. This syntax shows the easiest way to create a simple foreign key. After you run this statement, the DBMS will ensure that values inserted into the column *pub_id* in *titles* already exist in the column *pub_id* in *publishers*. Note that nulls aren't allowed in the foreign-key column, so every book must have a publisher.

```
CREATE TABLE titles
  (
  title_id   CHAR(3)      NOT NULL PRIMARY KEY,
  title_name VARCHAR(40)  NOT NULL            ,
  type       VARCHAR(10)                      ,
```

```
  pub_id      CHAR(3)       NOT NULL
    REFERENCES publishers(pub_id)                ,
  pages       INTEGER                            ,
  price       DECIMAL(5,2)                       ,
  sales       INTEGER                            ,
  pubdate     DATE                               ,
  contract    SMALLINT      NOT NULL
  );
```

DBMS To run the preceding example in **Microsoft SQL Server**, change the data type of the column *pubdate* to DATETIME.

The following example defines the column *title_id* to be both the primary key and a foreign key that points to *title_id* in *titles*.

```
CREATE TABLE royalties
  (
  title_id     CHAR(3)       NOT NULL,
  advance      DECIMAL(9,2)          ,
  royalty_rate DECIMAL(5,2)          ,
  CONSTRAINT royalties_pk
    PRIMARY KEY (title_id),
  CONSTRAINT royalties_title_id_fk
    FOREIGN KEY (title_id) REFERENCES titles(title_id)
  );
```

The following example uses named table constraints to create two foreign keys. This syntax shows the preferred way to add foreign keys; you can use the names if you decide to change or delete the keys later (page 186). Each foreign-key column is an individual key and *not* part of a single composite key. Note that foreign keys together, however, comprise the table's composite primary key.

```
CREATE TABLE title_authors
  (
  title_id      CHAR(3)      NOT NULL,
  au_id         CHAR(3)      NOT NULL,
  au_order      SMALLINT     NOT NULL,
  royalty_share DECIMAL(5,2) NOT NULL,
  CONSTRAINT title_authors_pk PRIMARY KEY (title_id, au_id),
  CONSTRAINT title_authors_fk1
    FOREIGN KEY (title_id) REFERENCES titles(title_id),
  CONSTRAINT title_authors_fk2
    FOREIGN KEY (au_id) REFERENCES authors(au_id)
  );
```

Tip: SQL lets you define the action the DBMS takes when you try to UPDATE or DELETE a key value (in a parent table) to which foreign-key values point. To trigger a referential action, specify an ON UPDATE or ON DELETE clause in the FOREIGN KEY constraint. Support for these clauses varies by DBMS; search your DBMS documentation for *foreign key* or *referential integrity.*

Preserving Referential Integrity

To preserve referential integrity, your DBMS won't let you create orphan rows or make existing rows **orphans** (rows in a foreign-key table without an associated row in a parent table). When you INSERT, UPDATE, or DELETE a row with a FOREIGN KEY column that references a PRIMARY KEY column in a parent table, your DBMS performs the following referential-integrity checks:

Inserting a row into the foreign-key table. The DBMS checks that the new FOREIGN KEY value matches a PRIMARY KEY value in the parent table. If no match exists, the DBMS won't INSERT the row.

Updating a row in the foreign-key table. The DBMS checks that the updated FOREIGN KEY value matches a PRIMARY KEY value in the parent table. If no match exists, the DBMS won't UPDATE the row.

Deleting a row in the foreign-key table. A referential-integrity check is unnecessary.

Inserting a row into the parent table. A referential-integrity check is unnecessary.

Updating a row in the parent table. The DBMS checks that none of the FOREIGN KEY values matches the PRIMARY KEY value to be updated. If a match exists, the DBMS won't UPDATE the row.

Deleting a row from the parent table. The DBMS checks that none of the FOREIGN KEY values matches the PRIMARY KEY value to be deleted. If a match exists, the DBMS won't DELETE the row.

The DBMS skips the referential-integrity check for rows with a null in the FOREIGN KEY column.

Forcing Unique Values with UNIQUE

A unique constraint ensures that a column (or set of columns) contains no duplicate values. A unique constraint is similar to a primary-key constraint (page 175), except that a unique column can contain nulls and a table can have multiple unique columns.

Suppose that you add the column *isbn* to the table *titles* to hold a book's ISBN. An ISBN is a unique, standardized identification number that marks a book unmistakably. *titles* already has a primary key (*title_id*), so to ensure that each ISBN value is unique, you define a unique constraint on the column *isbn*.

When you're defining a unique constraint, some important considerations are:

- A one-column key is a simple constraint; a multiple-column key is a composite constraint.
- In a composite constraint, values can be duplicated within one column, but each combination of values from all the columns must be unique.
- A simple unique constraint can be a column constraint or a table constraint; a composite unique constraint always is a table constraint (page 169).
- You define a unique constraint by using the keyword UNIQUE in a CREATE TABLE definition. A table can have zero or more unique constraints.
- As a table constraint, UNIQUE makes you specify column name(s). As a column constraint, UNIQUE applies to the column in which it's defined.
- In practice, unique constraints almost always are named explicitly. To name a constraint, use a CONSTRAINT clause (page 169).
- A UNIQUE column can forbid nulls with NOT NULL (page 171).

To specify a simple unique constraint as a column constraint, add the following column constraint to a CREATE TABLE column definition:

```
[CONSTRAINT constraint_name] UNIQUE
```

To specify a unique constraint as a table constraint, add the following table constraint to a CREATE TABLE definition:

```
[CONSTRAINT constraint_name] UNIQUE (unique_column)
```

For a composite unique constraint, specify a list of comma-separated column names in *unique_column* in the table constraint.

The following example uses a column constraint to designate a unique column. This syntax shows the easiest way to create a simple unique constraint.

```
CREATE TABLE titles
  (
  title_id   CHAR(3)      PRIMARY KEY    ,
  title_name VARCHAR(40)  NOT NULL UNIQUE,
  type       VARCHAR(10)                 ,
  pub_id     CHAR(3)      NOT NULL       ,
  pages      INTEGER                     ,
  price      DECIMAL(5,2)                ,
  sales      INTEGER                     ,
  pubdate    DATE                        ,
  contract   SMALLINT     NOT NULL
  );
```

DBMS To run the preceding example in **Microsoft SQL Server**, change the data type of the column *pubdate* to DATETIME.

The following example defines a multicolumn unique constraint for the sample-database table *authors*. This constraint forces the combination of each author's first and last name to be unique.

```
CREATE TABLE authors
  (
  au_id    CHAR(3)     NOT NULL,
  au_fname VARCHAR(15) NOT NULL,
  au_lname VARCHAR(15) NOT NULL,
  phone    VARCHAR(12)         ,
  address  VARCHAR(20)         ,
  city     VARCHAR(15)         ,
  state    CHAR(2)             ,
  zip      CHAR(5)             ,
  CONSTRAINT authors_pk
    PRIMARY KEY (au_id),
  CONSTRAINT authors_unique1
    UNIQUE (au_fname, au_lname)
  );
```

Tip: You can create a unique index (Chapter 22) instead of a unique constraint. To determine whether your DBMS prefers an index or a constraint, search your DBMS documentation for *unique*, *index*, or *constraint*.

Adding a Check Constraint with CHECK

So far, the only restrictions on an inserted value are that it have the proper data type, size, and range for its column. You can use check constraints to further limit the values that a column (or set of columns) accepts. Check constraints commonly are used to check the following:

Minimum or maximum values. Prevent sales of fewer than zero items, for example.

Specific values. Allow only 'biology', 'chemistry', or 'physics' in the column *science*, for example.

A range of values. Make sure that an author's royalty rate is between 2 percent and 20 percent, for example.

A check constraint determines the valid values by using a logical (Boolean) expression. The following check constraint, for example, ensures that no employee's salary exceeds $50000:

```
CHECK (salary <= 50000)
```

When you're defining a check constraint, some important considerations are:

- A check constraint that applies to a single column can be a column constraint or a table constraint; a check constraint that applies to multiple columns always is a table constraint (page 169).
- You define a check constraint by using the keyword CHECK in a CREATE TABLE definition.
- A column can have zero or more check constraints associated with it.
- If you create multiple check constraints for a column, design them carefully so that their purposes don't conflict. Don't assume that the DBMS will evaluate the constraints in any particular order or will verify that the constraints are mutually exclusive.
- In practice, check constraints almost always are named explicitly. To name a constraint, use a CONSTRAINT clause (page 169).
- The check constraint's condition is almost any valid WHERE condition, such as a comparison (=, <>, <, <=, >, >=), LIKE, BETWEEN, IN, or IS NULL condition. (Most DBMSs don't allow subqueries in check constraints.) You can join multiple conditions with AND, OR, or NOT.
- A check constraint's condition can refer to any column in the table, but it can't refer to columns in other tables.

To add a check constraint as a column constraint or table constraint, add the following constraint to a CREATE TABLE definition:

```
[CONSTRAINT constraint_name]
  CHECK (condition)
```

condition is a logical (Boolean) condition that the DBMS evaluates each time an INSERT, UPDATE, or DELETE statement modifies the contents of the table. If *condition* evaluates to true or unknown (due to a null) after the modification, the DBMS allows the change. If *condition* evaluates to false, the DBMS undoes the change and returns an error.

Tip: Although it's possible to add check constraints after a table has been populated with data, it's a better practice to impose check constraints before populating the table to detect input errors as early as possible.

The following example shows various column and table check constraints for the sample-database table *titles*. The constraint *title_id_chk* makes sure the each primary-key value takes the form 'T*nn*', in which *nn* represents an integer between 00 and 99, inclusive.

```
CREATE TABLE titles
  (
  title_id   CHAR(3)      NOT NULL,
  title_name VARCHAR(40)  NOT NULL,
  type       VARCHAR(10)
    CONSTRAINT type_chk
      CHECK (type IN ('biography','children','computer',
        'history','psychology'))   ,
  pub_id     CHAR(3)      NOT NULL,
  pages      INTEGER
    CHECK (pages > 0)              ,
  price      DECIMAL(5,2)          ,
  sales      INTEGER               ,
  pubdate    DATE                  ,
  contract   SMALLINT     NOT NULL,
  CONSTRAINT titles_pk PRIMARY KEY (title_id),
  CONSTRAINT titles_pub_id_fk
    FOREIGN KEY (pub_id) REFERENCES publishers(pub_id),
  CONSTRAINT title_id_chk
    CHECK (
    (SUBSTRING(title_id FROM 1 FOR 1) = 'T') AND
    (CAST(SUBSTRING(title_id FROM 2 FOR 2) AS INTEGER)
    BETWEEN 0 AND 99)),
```

```
  CONSTRAINT price_chk
    CHECK (price >= 0.00 AND price < 100.00),
  CONSTRAINT sales_chk
    CHECK (sales >= 0),
  CONSTRAINT pubdate_chk
    CHECK (pubdate >= DATE '1950-01-01'),
  CONSTRAINT title_name_chk
    CHECK (title_name <> '' AND contract >= 0),
  CONSTRAINT revenue_chk
    CHECK (price * sales >= 0.00)
  );
```

DBMS To run the preceding example in **Microsoft Access**, convert the two column constraints (for the columns *type* and *pages*) to table constraints by moving them after the last column definition. Change the first substring expression to Mid(title_id, 1, 1); change the CAST expression to CInt(Mid(title_id, 2, 2)); and drop the keyword DATE from the date literal and surround it with # characters instead of quotes (#1950-01-01#).

To run the preceding example in **Microsoft SQL Server**, change the data type of the column *pubdate* to DATETIME; change the two substring expressions to SUBSTRING(title_id, 1, 1) and SUBSTRING(title_id, 2, 2); and drop the keyword DATE from the date literal ('1950-01-01').

To run the preceding example in **Oracle**, change the two substring expressions to SUBSTR(title_id, 1, 1) and SUBSTR(title_id, 2, 2).

To run the preceding example in **DB2**, change the two substring expressions to SUBSTR(title_id, 1, 1) and SUBSTR(title_id, 2, 2) and drop the keyword DATE from the date literal ('1950-01-01').

MySQL doesn't support named CHECK column constraints, nor does it enforce check constraints. To run the preceding example, remove CONSTRAINT type_chk. Also, change the CAST data type from INTEGER to SIGNED.

In **Microsoft SQL Server**, you can specify the check constraint *title_id_chk* alternatively as CHECK (title_id LIKE '[T][0-9][0-9]'); search SQL Server Help for *pattern* or *wildcard*.

Tip: The SQL standard says that a check condition can't reference the datetime and user functions (CURRENT_TIMESTAMP, CURRENT_USER, and so on), but some DBMSs, such as **Microsoft Access**, **Microsoft SQL Server**, and **PostgreSQL**, allow them, for example: `CHECK(ship_time >= CURRENT_TIMESTAMP)`.

Altering a Table with ALTER TABLE

Use the ALTER TABLE statement to modify a table definition by adding, altering, or dropping columns and constraints.

DBMS Despite the SQL standard, the implementation of ALTER TABLE varies greatly by DBMS. To determine what you can alter and the conditions under which alterations are allowed, search your DBMS documentation for *alter table*. Depending on your DBMS, some of the modifications that you can make by using ALTER TABLE are:

- Add or drop a column
- Alter a column's data type
- Add, alter, or drop a column's default value or nullability constraint
- Add, alter, or drop column or table constraints such as primary-key, foreign-key, unique, and check constraints
- Rename a column
- Rename a table

To alter a table, type:

```
ALTER TABLE table
  alter_table_action;
```

table is the name of the table to alter. *alter_table_action* is a clause that specifies the action to take and begins with the keyword ADD, ALTER, or DROP. Some example actions are:

```
ADD COLUMN column type [constraints]
```

```
ALTER COLUMN column SET DEFAULT expr
```

```
DROP COLUMN column [RESTRICT|CASCADE]
```

```
ADD table_constraint
```

```
DROP CONSTRAINT constraint_name
```

The following examples add and drop the column *email_address* from the table *authors*.

```
ALTER TABLE authors
  ADD email_address CHAR(25);
```

```
ALTER TABLE authors
  DROP COLUMN email_address;
```

Tip: You can't drop a table's only remaining column.

To alter or drop a constraint, use the name that you specified in the CONSTRAINT clause when you created the constraint (page 169). If you didn't name the constraint, use the constraint name that your DBMS generated automatically.

DBMSs typically enforce fewer modification restrictions on empty tables than they do on populated tables. When you add a new column to a table that already has one or more rows, for example, that column can't have a NOT NULL constraint, whereas a new column in an empty table can be non-nullable.

Renaming Tables

Table renaming varies by DBMS. Table 21.2 lists the commands that rename tables in the current database. Renaming a table has no effect on its stored data.

Tip: Use caution when renaming a table. Changing the name can break SQL scripts and stored procedures. If there is a foreign key or view that references the table, attempts to rename it can cause an error.

Table 21.2 Renaming Tables

DBMS	Command
Access	Right-click a table in the Navigation pane and then click Rename
SQL Server	EXEC sp_rename '*old_name*', '*new_name*'
Oracle	RENAME *old_name* TO *new_name*;
DB2	RENAME TABLE *old_name* TO *new_name*;
MySQL	RENAME TABLE *old_name* TO *new_name*;
PostgreSQL	ALTER TABLE *old_name* RENAME TO *new_name*;

Dropping a Table with DROP TABLE

Use the DROP TABLE statement to remove a table from a database. When you're dropping a table, some important considerations are:

- Some DBMSs let you recover a dropped table by rolling back a transaction (Chapter 24). If a dropped table wasn't part of a transaction, you can restore the table from the most recent backup (though it might be out of date).
- Dropping a table destroys its structure, data, indexes, constraints, permissions, and so on.
- Dropping a table isn't the same as deleting all its rows. You can empty a table of rows, but not destroy it, with `DELETE FROM` *`table`*`;` (page 165).
- Dropping a table doesn't drop views (Chapter 23) that reference that table.
- You'll have problems with foreign keys or views that reference a dropped table unless they're altered or dropped as well.

To drop a table, type:

```
DROP TABLE table;
```

The following example drops the table *royalties*.

```
DROP TABLE royalties;
```

DBMS Some DBMSs make you drop or alter certain other properties before dropping the table itself. In **Microsoft SQL Server**, for example, you can't use DROP TABLE to drop a table referenced by a FOREIGN KEY constraint until the referencing FOREIGN KEY constraint or the referencing table is dropped first.

Standard SQL lets you specify RESTRICT or CASCADE drop behavior. RESTRICT (which is safe) prevents you from dropping a table that's referenced by views or other constraints. CASCADE (which is dangerous) causes referencing objects to be dropped along with the table. To find out whether your DBMS supports this feature or a similar one, search your DBMS documentation for *drop table*.

CHAPTER 22

Indexes

Understanding Indexes

Recall from “Tables” on page 8 that rows stored in a table are unordered, as required by the relational model. This lack of order makes it easy for the DBMS to INSERT, UPDATE, and DELETE rows quickly, but its unfortunate side effect is that it makes searching and sorting inefficient. Suppose that you run this query:

```
SELECT *
  FROM authors
  WHERE au_lname = 'Hull';
```

To execute this query, the DBMS must search the entire table *authors* sequentially, comparing the value in each row’s *au_lname* column to the string *Hull*. Searching an entire table in a small database is trivial, but production database tables can have millions of rows.

DBMSs provide a mechanism called an **index** that has the same purpose as its book or library counterpart: speeding data retrieval. At a simplified level, an index is a sorted list in which every distinct value in an indexed column (or set of columns) is stored with the disk address (physical location) of the rows containing that value. Instead of reading an entire table to locate specific rows, the DBMS scans only the index for addresses to access directly. Indexed searches typically are orders of magnitude faster than sequential searches, but some tradeoffs are involved, as explained in this chapter.

Indexes are complex; their design and effects on performance depend on the idiosyncrasies of your DBMS's optimizer. This section provides guidelines, but search your DBMS documentation for *index* to learn how your DBMS implements and uses indexes. In general, indexes are *appropriate* for columns that are frequently:

- Searched (WHERE)
- Sorted (ORDER BY)
- Grouped (GROUP BY)
- Used in joins (JOIN)
- Used to calculate order statistics (MIN(), MAX(), or the median, for example)

In general, indexes are *inappropriate* for columns that:

- Accept only a few distinct values (*gender*, *state*, or *marital_status*, for example)
- Are used rarely in queries
- Are part of a small table with few rows

When you're creating an index, some important considerations are:

- SQL's indexing statements modify database objects, so your database administrator might need to grant you permission to run them.
- An index never changes data; it's merely a fast access path to the data.
- A table can have zero or more indexes.
- Ideally, you create all a table's indexes when you create the table. In practice, index management is an iterative process. Typically, only vital indexes are created along with the table. Other indexes are added or deleted over time as performance problems grow or ebb and users' access patterns change. DBMSs provide testing and benchmarking tools to determine the effectiveness of indexes.
- Don't create any more indexes than you need. The DBMS must update (and possibly reorganize) an index after you INSERT, UPDATE, or DELETE rows in a table (see Chapters 19 and 20). As the number of indexes on a table grows, row-modification performance degrades as the DBMS spends more and more time maintaining indexes. In general, you shouldn't create more than about a dozen indexes for a table.

- Your DBMS will maintain and use indexes automatically after they're created. No additional actions are required by users or SQL programmers to reflect data changes in all relevant indexes.
- Indexes are transparent to the user and SQL programmer. The absence or presence of an index doesn't require a change in the wording of any SQL statement.
- An index can reference one or more columns in a table. An index that references a single column is a **simple index**; an index that references multiple columns is a **composite index**. Columns in a composite index need not be adjacent in the table. A single index can't span multiple tables.
- The order in which columns appear in a composite index is significant. A composite index applies only to the group of columns on which it's defined, not to each column individually or the same columns in different order.
- You can create multiple composite indexes that use the same columns if you specify distinctly different combinations of the columns. The following two statements, for example, specify valid combinations for the same table:

  ```
  CREATE INDEX au_name_idx1 ON authors (au_fname, au_lname);
  CREATE INDEX au_name_idx2 ON authors (au_lname, au_fname);
  ```

- In addition to allowing rapid sorts and searches, an index can ensure uniqueness. A **unique index** forces the value of the column (or columns) upon which the index is based to be distinct in the table. If you try to create a unique index for column(s) in which duplicate values already exist, your DBMS will generate an error and refuse to create the index. DBMSs create unique indexes automatically when you define a primary-key constraint or unique constraint.
- A DBMS may or may not create indexes for foreign keys automatically. If not, you should create these indexes yourself, because most joins involve a foreign key.
- All DBMSs implement indexes even though indexes aren't part of the relational model (and don't violate any of the model's rules).

Creating an Index with CREATE INDEX

Indexes aren't part of the SQL standard, so index-related SQL statements vary by DBMS, although the syntax for the minimal CREATE INDEX statement is the same for the DBMSs covered in this book.

To create an index, type:

```
CREATE [UNIQUE] INDEX index
  ON table (index_columns);
```

index is the name of the index to create and is a valid SQL identifier (page 20). Index names must be unique within a table. For **Oracle**, **DB2**, and **PostgreSQL**, index names must be unique within a database.

table is the name of the table to create the index for, and *index_columns* is a list of one or more comma-separated names of the columns to index.

Specify UNIQUE to create a unique index. UNIQUE causes the DBMS to check for duplicates in *index_columns*. If *table* already contains rows with duplicates in *index_columns*, the DBMS won't create the index. If you attempt to INSERT or UPDATE duplicate values in unique *index_columns*, the DBMS generates an error and cancels the operation.

The following CREATE INDEX statement creates a simple index named *pub_id_idx* on the column *pub_id* for the table *titles*. *pub_id* is a foreign key and is a good candidate for an index because:

- Changes to PRIMARY KEY constraints are checked with FOREIGN KEY constraints in related tables.
- Foreign-key columns often are used in join criteria when the data from related tables are combined in queries by matching the FOREIGN KEY column(s) of one table with the PRIMARY KEY or UNIQUE column(s) in the other table.

```
CREATE INDEX pub_id_idx
  ON titles (pub_id);
```

The following CREATE INDEX statement creates a simple unique index named *title_name_idx* on the column *title_name* for the table *titles*. The DBMS will create this index only if no duplicates already exist in the column *title_name*. This index also prohibits nondistinct title names from being INSERTed or UPDATEd in *titles*.

```
CREATE UNIQUE INDEX title_name_idx
  ON titles (title_name);
```

The following CREATE INDEX statement creates a composite index named *state_city_idx* on the columns *state* and *city* for the table *authors*. The DBMS uses this index when you sort rows in *state* plus *city* order. This index is useless for sorts and searches on *state* alone, *city* alone, or *city* plus *state*; you must create separate indexes for those purposes.

```
CREATE INDEX state_city_idx
  ON authors (state, city);
```

Tips for CREATE INDEX

- Don't use the terms *index* and *key* interchangeably. An index is a *physical* (hardware-related) mechanism that the DBMS uses to improve performance. A key is a *logical* (based on data) concept that the DBMS uses to enforce referential integrity and update through views.
- You also can use a UNIQUE constraint (page 181) to prevent duplicate column values.
- Indexes are files stored on disk and so occupy storage space (possibly a lot of space). But when used properly, indexes are the primary means of reducing disk wear and tear by obviating the need to read large tables sequentially. While a DBMS is creating an index, it uses as much as 1.5 times the space that the associated table occupies (make sure you have room). Most of that space is released after the index is complete.
- Searching a table sequentially (for lack of an index) is called a **table scan**.
- A **clustered index** is an index in which the logical order of the key values determines the physical order of the corresponding rows in a table. In a **nonclustered index**, the index's logical order differs from the physical, stored order of the on-disk rows. A table can have at most one clustered index. Clustered indexes usually improve performance, but in some cases they make searches much faster but INSERTs, UPDATEs, and DELETEs much slower.
- Most indexes are implemented as **balanced trees**, or **B-trees**. A B-tree is an advanced data structure that minimizes disk read/write operations. Some DBMSs let you specify the data structure to use when constructing an index.
- DBMS **Microsoft SQL Server** and **DB2** consider multiple nulls to be duplicates when UNIQUE is specified and allow no more than one null in columns with a unique index. **Microsoft Access**, **Oracle**, **MySQL**, and **PostgreSQL** allow multiple nulls in such columns.

Dropping an Index with DROP INDEX

Use the DROP INDEX statement to destroy an index. Because an index is logically and physically independent of the data in its associated table, you can drop the index at any time without affecting the table (or other indexes). All SQL programs and other applications will continue to work if you drop an index, but access to previously indexed data will be slower.

The usual reasons for dropping an index are:

- The index is no longer needed because the associated table is much smaller (or was dropped), or users don't access the index's columns much anymore.
- The extra time it takes the DBMS to maintain the index after INSERT, UPDATE, or DELETE operations outweighs the speed improvement in retrieval operations that the index provides.

DBMS The SQL standard omits indexes, so index-related SQL statements vary by DBMS. This section describes how to drop an index for each DBMS covered in this book. If you're using a different DBMS, search the documentation for *index* to learn how to drop an index.

In **Oracle**, **DB2**, and **PostgreSQL**, index names must be unique within a database, so you don't specify a table name when you drop an index. In **Microsoft Access**, **Microsoft SQL Server**, and **MySQL**, index names must be unique within a table but can be reused in other tables, so you must specify a table along with the index to be dropped.

To drop an index in **Microsoft Access** or **MySQL**, type:

```
DROP INDEX index ON table;
```

To drop an index in **Microsoft SQL Server**, type:

```
DROP INDEX table.index;
```

To drop an index in **Oracle**, **DB2**, or **PostgreSQL**, type:

```
DROP INDEX index;
```

The following equivalent forms of DROP INDEX drop the index *pub_id_idx*.

```
DROP INDEX pub_id_idx ON titles;  -- Microsoft Access, MySQL
DROP INDEX titles.pub_id_idx;     -- Microsoft SQL Server
DROP INDEX pub_id_idx;            -- Oracle, DB2, PostgreSQL
```

Tip: You can't drop indexes that the DBMS creates automatically for PRIMARY KEY and UNIQUE constraints (Chapter 21).

CHAPTER 23

Views

Understanding Views

A **view** is a stored SELECT statement that returns a table whose data are derived from one or more other tables (called **underlying tables**). Some important characteristics of a view are:

- A view's underlying tables can be base tables or other views.
- A view is called a **virtual table** or **derived table** to distinguish it from a base table.
- The DBMS stores a view as *only* a SELECT statement, *not* as a set of data values, thus preventing data redundancy.
- A view materializes dynamically as a physical table when referenced by name in an SQL statement. It exists only for the duration of the statement and vanishes when the statement finishes.
- A view is a set of named columns and rows of data, so you can use it almost anywhere you'd use a real table.
- You have no restrictions on querying (SELECTing) through views. In some cases, views can be updated, causing the data changes to be passed through to the underlying base tables.
- Because of closure (page 9), a view always is a single table no matter how many underlying tables it references or how those tables are combined.

Think of a view as being a tailored presentation that provides a tabular window into one or more base tables. The window can display an entire base table, part of a base table, or a combination of base tables (or parts thereof). A view also can reflect the data in base tables through other views—windows into windows. Generally, SQL programmers use views to present data to end-users in database applications. Views offer these advantages:

Simplified data access. Views hide data complexity and simplify statements, so users can perform operations on a view more easily than on the base tables directly. If you create a complex view—one that involves, say, multiple base tables, joins, and subqueries—users can query this view without having to understand complex relational concepts or even knowing that multiple tables are involved.

Automatic updating. When a base table is updated, all views that reference the table reflect the change automatically. If you insert a row representing a new author into the table *authors*, for example, all views defined over *authors* will reflect the new author automatically. This scheme saves disk space and prevents redundancy because, without views, the DBMS would have to store derived data to keep it synchronized.

Increased security. One of the most common uses of views is to hide data from users by filtering the underlying tables. Suppose that the table *employees* contains the columns *salary* and *commission*. If you create a view on *employees* that omits these two columns but contains other innocuous columns (such as *email_address*), the database administrator can grant users permission to see the view but not see the underlying table, thereby hiding compensation data from the curious.

Logical data independence. Base tables provide a **real view** of a database. But when you use SQL to build a database application, you want to present end users not the real view, but a **virtual view** specific to the application. The virtual view hides the parts of the database (entire tables or specific rows or columns) that aren't relevant to the application. Thus, users interact with the virtual view, which is derived from—though independent of—the real view presented by the base tables.

A virtual view immunizes an application from logical changes in the design of the database. Suppose that many applications access the table *titles*. Books go out of print over time, so the database designer decides to reduce the system load by segregating out-of-print books. He splits *titles* into two tables: *in_print_titles* and *out_of_print_titles*. Consequently, all the applications break because they expect the now-unavailable table *titles*.

But if those applications had accessed a *view* of *titles* instead of the real table, that view could be redefined to be the UNION (Chapter 18) of *in_print_titles* and *out_of_print_titles*. The applications transparently would see the two new tables as though they were the one original table and continue to work as though the split never happened. (You can't use views to immunize an application against *all* changes, however. Views can't compensate for dropped tables or columns, for example.)

When you're creating a view, some important considerations are:

- View-related SQL statements modify database objects and data, so your database administrator might need to grant you permission to run them.
- View names follow the same rules that table names do.
- View names must be unique within a database. They can't have the same name as any other table or view.
- The columns in a view inherit the default column names from the underlying tables. You can give view columns different names by using AS (page 28).
- You must specify a new name for a column in a view that would have the same name as another column in the view (usually because the view definition includes a join and the columns from two or more different underlying tables have the same name).
- A column defined in a view can be a simple column reference, a literal, or an expression that involves calculations or aggregate functions.
- In some DBMSs, you must specify explicitly the name of a column in a view if the column is derived from an arithmetic expression, a built-in function, or a literal.
- A view column inherits the data type of the column or expression from which it is derived.
- You have no practical limit on the number of views that you can create. Generally, you want to create views on subsets of data that are of interest to many users.
- Almost any valid SELECT statement can define a view, though an ORDER BY clause usually is prohibited.
- You can nest views—that is, a view's SELECT statement can retrieve data from another view. Nested views eventually must resolve to base tables (otherwise, you'd be viewing nothing). The maximum number of nesting levels varies by DBMS.

- You can use views as a convenience to save complex queries. By saving a query that performs extensive calculations as a view, you can recalculate each time the view is queried.
- A view can express a query that you'd otherwise be unable to run. You can define a view that joins a GROUP BY view with a base table, for example, or define a view that joins a UNION view with a base table.
- A view definition can't reference itself, because it doesn't exist yet.
- Views can display data formatted differently from those in the underlying tables.
- Unlike a base table, a view doesn't support constraints. Some DBMSs let you index views.
- When you define a view by using SELECT *, SQL converts the * to a list of all columns internally. This conversion occurs only once, at view creation (not at execution), so the definition of your view won't change if someone adds a column to an underlying table (by using ALTER TABLE).
- Because views store no data, the DBMS must execute them every time they're referenced. Complex views—particularly nested views—can degrade performance seriously.

Creating a View with CREATE VIEW

To create a view, type:

```
CREATE VIEW view [(view_columns)]
  AS select_query;
```

view is the name of the view to create. The view name must be unique within the database.

view_columns is an optional, parenthesized list of one or more comma-separated names to be used for the columns in *view*. The number of columns in *view_columns* must match the number of columns in the SELECT clause of *select_query*. (If you name one column this way, you must name them all this way.) Specify *view_columns* when a column in *select_query* is derived from an arithmetic expression, a function, or a literal; when two or more view columns would otherwise have the same name (usually because of a join); or to give a column in view a name different from that of the column from which it was derived. If *view_columns* is omitted, *view* inherits column names from *select_query*. Column names also can be assigned in *select_query* via AS clauses. Each column name must be unique within the view.

select_query is a SELECT query that identifies the columns and rows of the table(s) that the view is based on. *select_query* can be arbitrarily complex and use more than one table or other views. An ORDER BY clause usually is prohibited. For DBMS-specific restrictions on SELECT in views, search your DBMS's documentation for *CREATE VIEW*.

The following example creates a view that hides the authors' personal information (telephone numbers and addresses).

```
CREATE VIEW au_names AS
  SELECT au_id, au_fname, au_lname
    FROM authors;
```

The following example creates a view that lists the authors who live in a city in which a publisher is located. Note that I use the column names *au_city* and *pub_city* in the view. Renaming these columns resolves the ambiguity that would arise if both columns inherited the same column name *city* from the underlying tables.

```
CREATE VIEW cities (au_id, au_city, pub_id, pub_city) AS
  SELECT a.au_id, a.city, p.pub_id, p.city
    FROM authors a
    INNER JOIN publishers p
      ON a.city = p.city;
```

The following example creates a view that lists total revenue (= price × sales) grouped by book type within publisher. The result of the arithmetic expression (*Revenue*) is named explicitly.

```
CREATE VIEW revenues (Publisher, BookType, Revenue) AS
  SELECT pub_id, type, SUM(price * sales)
    FROM titles
    GROUP BY pub_id, type;
```

The following example creates a view that lists the last names of authors A02 and A05, and the books that each one wrote (or cowrote). Note that this statement uses a nested view: it references the view *au_names* created above.

```
CREATE VIEW au_titles (LastName, Title) AS
  SELECT an.au_lname, t.title_name
    FROM title_authors ta
    INNER JOIN au_names an
      ON ta.au_id = an.au_id
    INNER JOIN titles t
      ON t.title_id = ta.title_id
    WHERE an.au_id in ('A02','A05');
```

DBMS When you run a CREATE VIEW statement in **Microsoft Access**, the view appears as a query object in the Database window. To run the preceding example in Access, nest the joins:

```
CREATE VIEW au_titles (LastName, Title) AS
  SELECT an.au_lname, t.title_name
    FROM au_names an
    INNER JOIN (titles t
      INNER JOIN title_authors ta
        ON t.title_id = ta.title_id)
      ON an.au_id = ta.au_id
    WHERE an.au_id IN ('A02','A05');
```

To run a CREATE VIEW statement in **Microsoft SQL Server**, remove the terminating semicolon.

MySQL 5.0 and later support views. Earlier versions can't run the examples in this chapter.

Tip: Standard SQL has no ALTER VIEW statement. If the underlying table(s) or view(s) have changed since a view was created, then drop and re-create the view. **Microsoft SQL Server**, **Oracle**, **DB2**, **MySQL**, and **PostgreSQL**, however, support a nonstandard ALTER VIEW statement.

Using Check Options with Views

In **Microsoft SQL Server**, **Oracle**, **DB2**, **MySQL**, and **PostgreSQL**, you can add the optional clause WITH [CASCADED | LOCAL] CHECK OPTION when you create a view. This clause applies to only updateable views and ensures that only data that can be read by the view can be inserted, updated, or deleted. If a view shows authors from only New York state, for example, it would be impossible to insert, update, or delete non–New York authors through that view. The CASCADED and LOCAL options apply to nested views only. CASCADED performs the check for the current view and all the views it references. LOCAL performs the check for the current view only.

Retrieving Data Through a View

Creating a view displays nothing. All that CREATE VIEW does is cause the DBMS to save the view as a named SELECT statement. To see data through a view, query the view by using SELECT. All the SELECT clauses (FROM, WHERE, GROUP BY, JOIN, and so on) work with views the same way that they work with tables.

The following example queries the view *revenues* (created in the preceding section) to list the types of books whose average revenue exceeds $1 million.

```
SELECT BookType, AVG(Revenue) AS "AVG(Revenue)"
  FROM revenues
  GROUP BY BookType
  HAVING AVG(Revenue) > 1000000;
```

The result is:

```
BookType   AVG(Revenue)
---------  ------------
biography  18727318.50
computer    1025396.65
psychology 2320933.76
```

Updating Data Through a View

An **updateable view** is a view to which you can apply INSERT, UPDATE, and DELETE operations to modify data in the underlying table(s). Any changes made in an updateable view always pass through to the base table(s) unambiguously. The syntax for the INSERT, UPDATE, and DELETE statements is the same for views as it is for tables; see Chapters 19 and 20.

A **nonupdateable view** (or **read-only view**) view is one that doesn't support INSERT, UPDATE, and DELETE operations because changes would be ambiguous. To change the data that appear in a read-only view, you must change the underlying table(s) directly (or through another, nonambiguous view).

Each row in an updateable view is associated with exactly one row in an underlying base table. A view isn't updateable if its SELECT statement uses GROUP BY, HAVING, DISTINCT, or aggregate functions, for example.

The SQL-92 standard said that an updateable view must be defined over only one table, which is stringent but very safe. The SQL:1999 standard relaxed that restriction because many more types of updateable views exist. By the time that standard was released, the DBMS vendors already offered an expanded set of updateable views. Single-table views always are updateable. DBMSs also examine the underlying tables' joins and referential-integrity constraints of a multitable view to determine whether the view is updateable. The types of queries that can define updateable views include inner joins, outer joins, and UNIONs. An updateable view must contain a key of the base table to ensure that each view row maps back to only one row in the base table. See your DBMS documentation to find out which multitable views you can update and how those updates affect each base table.

View updates can have integrity repercussions, of course. The DBMS will disallow a deletion if removing a row violates a referential-integrity constraint; see "Specifying a Foreign Key with FOREIGN KEY" on page 177. If you delete a row, all the underlying FOREIGN KEY constraints in related tables must still be satisfied for the deletion to succeed. Some updating can be handled by the CASCADE option (if specified) of a FOREIGN KEY constraint, not by the view definition.

Dropping a View with DROP VIEW

Use the DROP VIEW statement to destroy a view. Because a view is physically independent of its underlying table(s), you can drop the view at any time without affecting the table(s). All SQL programs, applications, and other views that reference the dropped view will break, however.

To drop a view, type:

```
DROP VIEW view;
```

The following example drops the view *revenues*.

```
DROP VIEW revenues;
```

Tip: Dropping a base table (page 188) doesn't drop the views that reference that table, so you must drop the views with DROP VIEW explicitly.

CHAPTER 24

Transactions

Understanding Transactions

A **transaction** is a sequence of one or more SQL statements executed as a single logical unit of work. The DBMS considers a transaction to be an indivisible, all-or-nothing proposition: it executes all the transaction's statements as a group, or it executes none of them.

For example, suppose that a bank customer transfers $500 from her savings account to her checking account. This operation consists of two separate actions, executed sequentially:

1 Decrement savings balance by $500.

2 Increment checking balance by $500.

The two SQL statements for this transaction are:

```
UPDATE savings_accounts
  SET balance = balance - 500.00
  WHERE account_number = 208998628;

UPDATE checking_accounts
  SET balance = balance + 500.00
  WHERE account_number = 786783165;
```

Now imagine that the DBMS fails—power outage, system crash, hardware problem—after it executes the first statement but before the second. The accounts would be out of balance without your knowledge. Accusations of malfeasance and prison time would soon follow.

To avoid legal problems, use a transaction to guarantee that both SQL statements are performed to maintain the accounts in proper balance. When something prevents one of the statements in a transaction from executing, the DBMS undoes (rolls back) the other statements of the transaction. If no error occurs, the changes are made permanent (committed).

Executing a Transaction

To learn how transactions work, you need to learn a few terms:

Commit. Committing a transaction makes all data modifications performed since the start of the transaction a permanent part of the database. After a transaction is committed, all changes made by the transaction become visible to other users and are guaranteed to be permanent if a crash or other failure occurs.

Roll back. Rolling back a transaction retracts any of the changes resulting from the SQL statements in the transaction. After a transaction is rolled back, the affected data are left unchanged, as though the SQL statements in the transaction were never executed.

Transaction log. The **transaction log file**, or just **log**, is a serial record of all modifications that have occurred in a database via transactions. The transaction log records the start of each transaction, the changes to the data, and enough information to undo or redo the changes made by the transaction (if necessary later). The log grows continually as transactions occur in the database.

Although it's the DBMS's responsibility to ensure the *physical* integrity of each transaction, it's your responsibility to start and end transactions at points that enforce the *logical* consistency of the data, according to the rules of your organization or business. A transaction should contain only the SQL statements necessary to make a consistent change—no more and no fewer. Data in all referenced tables must be in a consistent state before the transaction begins and after it ends.

When you're designing and executing transactions, some important considerations are:

- Transaction-related SQL statements modify data, so your database administrator might need to grant you permission to run them.
- Transaction processing applies to statements that change data or database objects (INSERT, UPDATE, DELETE, CREATE, ALTER, DROP—the list varies by DBMS). For production databases, every such statement should be executed as part of a transaction.
- A committed transaction is said to be **durable**, meaning that its changes remain in place permanently, persisting even if the system fails.
- A DBMS's data-recovery mechanism depends on transactions. When the DBMS is brought back online following a failure, the DBMS checks its transaction log to see whether all transactions were committed to the database. If it finds uncommitted (partially executed) transactions, it rolls them back based on the log. You must resubmit the rolled-back transactions (although some DBMSs can complete unfinished transactions automatically).
- A DBMS's backup/restore facility depends on transactions. The backup facility takes regular snapshots of the database and stores them with (subsequent) transaction logs on a backup disk. Suppose that a crash damages a production disk in a way that renders the data and transaction log unreadable. You can invoke the restore facility, which will use the most recent database backup and then execute, or **roll forward**, all *committed* transactions in the log from the time the snapshot was taken to the last transaction preceding the failure. This restore operation brings the database to its correct state before the crash. (Again, you'll have to resubmit uncommitted transactions.)
- For obvious reasons, you should store a database and its transaction log on separate physical disks.

For a transaction to be executed in all-or-nothing fashion, the transaction's boundaries (starting and ending points) must be clear. These boundaries let the DBMS execute the statements as one atomic unit of work. A transaction can start **implicitly** with the first executable SQL statement or **explicitly** with the START TRANSACTION statement. A transaction ends explicitly with a COMMIT or ROLLBACK statement (it never ends implicitly). You can't roll back a transaction after you commit it.

DBMS **Oracle** and **DB2** transactions always start implicitly, so those DBMSs have no statement that marks the start of a transaction. In **Microsoft Access**, **Microsoft SQL Server**, **MySQL**, and **PostgreSQL**, you can (or must) start a transaction explicitly by using the BEGIN statement. The SQL:1999 standard introduced the START TRANSACTION statement—long after these DBMSs already were using BEGIN to start transactions, so the extended BEGIN syntax varies by DBMS. **MySQL** and **PostgreSQL** support START TRANSACTION (as a synonym for BEGIN).

To start a transaction explicitly in **Microsoft Access** or **Microsoft SQL Server**, type:

```
BEGIN TRANSACTION;
```

To start a transaction explicitly in **MySQL** or **PostgreSQL**, type:

```
START TRANSACTION;
```

To commit a transaction, type:

```
COMMIT;
```

To roll back a transaction, type:

```
ROLLBACK;
```

The following SELECT statements show that the UPDATE operations are performed by the DBMS and then undone by a ROLLBACK statement. Within a transaction block, UPDATE operations (like INSERT and DELETE operations) are never final.

```
SELECT SUM(pages), AVG(price) FROM titles;

BEGIN TRANSACTION;
  UPDATE titles SET pages = 0;
  UPDATE titles SET price = price * 2;
  SELECT SUM(pages), AVG(price) FROM titles;
ROLLBACK;

SELECT SUM(pages), AVG(price) FROM titles;
```

The results of the SELECT statements show that the DBMS cancelled the transaction:

```
SUM(pages) AVG(price)
---------- ----------
      5107    18.3875

SUM(pages) AVG(price)
---------- ----------
         0    36.7750

SUM(pages) AVG(price)
---------- ----------
      5107    18.3875
```

The following example shows a more practical example of a transaction. I want to delete the publisher P04 from the table *publishers* without generating a referential-integrity error. Because some of the foreign-key values in *titles* point to publisher P04 in *publishers*, I first need to delete the related rows from the tables *titles*, *titles_authors*, and *royalties*. I use a transaction to be certain that *all* the DELETE statements are executed. If only some of the statements were successful, the data would be left inconsistent. (For information about referential-integrity checks, see "Specifying a Foreign Key with FOREIGN KEY" on page 177.)

```
BEGIN TRANSACTION;

  DELETE FROM title_authors
    WHERE title_id IN
      (SELECT title_id
         FROM titles
         WHERE pub_id = 'P04');

  DELETE FROM royalties
    WHERE title_id IN
      (SELECT title_id
         FROM titles
         WHERE pub_id = 'P04');

  DELETE FROM titles
    WHERE pub_id = 'P04';

  DELETE FROM publishers
    WHERE pub_id = 'P04';

COMMIT;
```

DBMS In **Microsoft Access**, you can't execute transactions in a SQL View window or via DAO; you must use the Microsoft Jet OLE DB Provider and ADO.

Oracle and **DB2** transactions begin implicitly. To run the preceding examples in Oracle and DB2, omit the statement `BEGIN TRANSACTION;`.

To run the preceding examples in **MySQL**, change the statement `BEGIN TRANSACTION;` to `START TRANSACTION;` (or to `BEGIN;`).

Concurrency Control

To humans, computers appear to carry out two or more processes at the same time. In reality, computer operations occur not concurrently, but in sequence. The illusion of simultaneity appears because a microprocessor works with much smaller time slices than people can perceive. In a DBMS, **concurrency control** is a group of strategies that prevents loss of data integrity caused by interference between two or more users trying to access or change the same data simultaneously.

DBMSs use locking strategies to ensure transactional integrity and database consistency. **Locking** restricts data access during read and write operations; thus, it prevents users from reading data that are being changed by other users and prevents multiple users from changing the same data at the same time. Without locking, data can become logically incorrect, and statements executed against those data can return unexpected results. Occasionally you'll end up in a **deadlock**, where you and another user, each having locked a piece of data needed for the other's transaction, attempt to get a lock on each other's piece. Most DBMSs can detect and resolve deadlocks by rolling back one user's transaction so that the other can proceed (otherwise, you'd both wait forever for the other to release the lock). Locking mechanisms are very sophisticated; search your DBMS documentation for *locking*.

Concurrency transparency is the appearance from a transaction's perspective that it's the only transaction operating on the database. A DBMS isolates a transaction's changes from changes made by any other concurrent transactions. Consequently, a transaction never sees data in an intermediate state; either it sees data in the state they were in before another concurrent transaction changed them, or it sees the data after the other transaction has completed. Isolated transactions let you reload starting data and replay (roll forward) a series of transactions to end up with the data in the same state they were in after the original transactions were executed.

MySQL supports transactions through InnoDB and BDB tables; search the MySQL documentation for *transactions*.

Microsoft SQL Server, **Oracle**, **MySQL**, and **PostgreSQL** support the statement SET TRANSACTION to set the characteristics of the upcoming transaction. **DB2** transaction characteristics are controlled via server-level and connection initialization settings.

Tips for Transactions

- Don't forget to end transactions explicitly with either COMMIT or ROLLBACK. A missing endpoint could lead to huge transactions with unpredictable results on the data or, on abnormal program termination, rollback of the last uncommitted transaction. Keep your transactions as small as possible because they can lock rows, entire tables, indexes, and other resources for their duration. COMMIT or ROLLBACK releases the resources for other transactions.
- You can nest transactions. The maximum number of nesting levels depends on the DBMS.
- It's faster to UPDATE multiple columns with a single SET clause than to use multiple UPDATEs. For example, the query

  ```
  UPDATE mytable
    SET col1 = 1
        col2 = 2
        col3 = 3
    WHERE col1 <> 1
       OR col2 <> 2
       OR col3 <> 3;
  ```

  is better than three UPDATE statements because it decreases logging (although it increases locking).
- By default, DBMSs run in **autocommit mode** unless overridden by either explicit or implicit transactions (or turned off with a system setting). In this mode, each statement is executed as its own transaction. If a statement completes successfully, the DBMS commits it; if the DBMS encounters any error, it rolls back the statement.
- For long transactions, you can set arbitrary intermediate markers, called **savepoints**, to divide a transaction into smaller parts. Savepoints let you roll back changes made from the current point in the transaction to a location earlier in the transaction (provided that the transaction hasn't been committed). Imagine a session in which you've made a

complex series of uncommitted INSERTs, UPDATEs, and DELETEs and then realize that the last few changes are incorrect or unnecessary. You can use savepoints to avoid resubmitting every statement. **Microsoft Access** doesn't support savepoints. For **Oracle**, **DB2**, **MySQL**, and **PostgreSQL**, use the statement

```
SAVEPOINT savepoint_name;
```

For **Microsoft SQL Server**, use the statement

```
SAVE TRANSACTION savepoint_name;
```

See your DBMS documentation for information about savepoint locking subtleties and how to COMMIT or ROLLBACK to a particular savepoint.

ACID

ACID is an acronym that summarizes the properties of a transaction:

Atomicity. Either all of a transaction's data modifications are performed, or none of them are.

Consistency. A completed transaction leaves all data in a consistent state that maintains all data integrity. A consistent state satisfies all defined database constraints. (Note that consistency isn't necessarily preserved at any intermediate point *within* a transaction.)

Isolation. A transaction's effects are isolated (or concealed) from those of all other transactions. See the "Concurrency Control" sidebar earlier in this chapter.

Durability. After a transaction completes, its effects are permanent and persist even if the system fails.

Transaction theory is a big topic, separate from the relational model. A good reference is *Transaction Processing: Concepts and Techniques* by Jim Gray and Andreas Reuter (Morgan Kaufmann).

Appendix A

The Sample Database

If you want to follow along with the examples in this book, you can create the sample database on your DBMS. This appendix describes the database's main tables, how they're related to each other, and how to get them. (To run SQL programs on your DBMS, see Appendix B.)

The examples in this book use the sample database named *books*. Here are some things that you should know about *books*:

- Recall from "Tables" on page 8 that a database appears to the user as a collection of tables (and nothing but tables). *books* contains five main tables that contain information about authors, titles they've published, their publishers, and their royalties. The accompanying figure depicts these related tables (PK denotes a primary key).
- Some of the examples modify data in *books* (rather than just retrieve data). Unless I note otherwise, each new section in a chapter starts with a pristine copy of *books*. In other words, assume that database changes made in one section don't carry over to the next section.
- *books* is a teaching tool; its structure and size don't approach the complexity of real production databases.

Creating the Sample Database

To create (or re-create) the database *books* on your own DBMS, visit the companion website *fehily.com*, click the Download link for this book, and then follow the onscreen instructions. Creating *books* is a two-step process:

1. Use your DBMS's built-in tools to create a new, blank database named *books*.
2. Run an SQL script that creates tables within *books* and populates them with data.

DBMS If you're using **Microsoft Access**, you don't run a script—you simply open an Access database file.

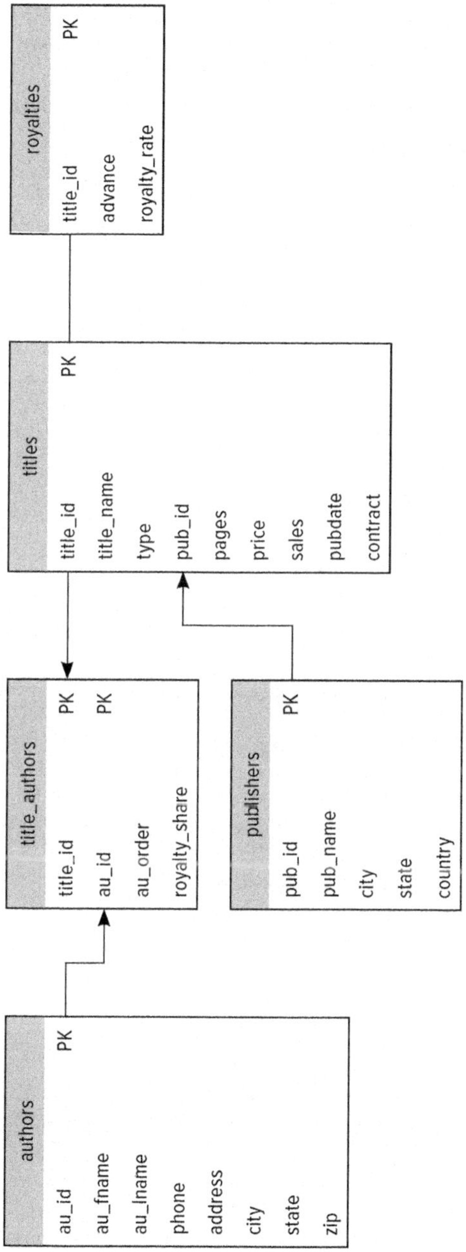
royalties
title_id PK
advance
royalty_rate
titles
title_id PK
title_name
type
pub_id
pages
price
sales
pubdate
contract
title_authors
title_id PK
au_id PK
au_order
royalty_share
publishers
pub_id PK
pub_name
city
state
country
authors
au_id PK
au_fname
au_lname
phone
address
city
state
zip

The table *authors*

The table *authors* describes the books' authors. Each author has a unique identifier (*au_id*) that's the primary key. Table A.1 shows the structure of the table *authors*.

The table *publishers*

The table *publishers* describes the books' publishers. Each publisher has a unique identifier (*pub_id*) that's the primary key. Table A.2 shows the structure of the table *publishers*.

Table A.1 Table Structure of *authors*

Column Name	Description	Data Type
au_id	Unique author identifier	CHAR(3)
au_fname	Author first name	VARCHAR(15)
au_lname	Author last name	VARCHAR(15)
phone	Author telephone number	VARCHAR(12)
address	Author address	VARCHAR(20)
city	Author city	VARCHAR(15)
state	Author state	CHAR(2)
zip	Author zip (postal) code	CHAR(5)

Table A.2 Table Structure of *publishers*

Column Name	Description	Data Type
pub_id	Unique publisher identifier	CHAR(3)
pub_name	Publisher name	VARCHAR(20)
city	Publisher city	VARCHAR(15)
state	Publisher state/province/region	CHAR(2)
country	Publisher country	VARCHAR(15)

The table *titles*

The table *titles* describes the books. Each book has a unique identifier (*title_id*) that's the primary key. *titles* contains a foreign key, *pub_id*, that references the table *publishers* to indicate a book's publisher. Table A.3 shows the structure of the table *titles*.

Table A.3 Table Structure of *titles*

Column Name	Description	Data Type
title_id	Unique title identifier	CHAR(3)
title_name	Book title	VARCHAR(40)
type	Subject of the book	VARCHAR(10)
pub_id	Publisher identifier	CHAR(3)
pages	Page count	INTEGER
price	Cover price	DECIMAL(5,2)
sales	Lifetime number of copies sold	INTEGER
pubdate	Date of publication	DATE
contract	Nonzero if author(s) signed contract	SMALLINT

The table *title_authors*

Authors and books have a many-to-many relationship, because an author can write multiple books and a book can have multiple authors. *title_authors* is the junction table that associates the tables *authors* and *titles*. *title_id* and *au_id* together form a composite primary key, and each column separately is a foreign key that references *titles* and *authors*, respectively. The non-key columns indicate the order of the author's name on the book's cover (always 1 for a book with a sole author) and the fraction of total royalties that each author receives (always 1.0 for a book with a sole author). Table A.4 shows the structure of the table *title_authors*.

The table *royalties*

The table *royalties* specifies the royalty rate paid to *all* the authors (not each author) of each book, including the total up-front advance against royalties paid to all authors (again, not each author) of a book. The *royalties* primary key is *title_id*. The table *royalties* has a one-to-one relationship with *titles*, so the *royalties* primary key also is a foreign key that references the *titles* primary key. Table A.5 shows the structure of the table *royalties*.

Table A.4 Table Structure of *title_authors*

Column Name	Description	Data Type
title_id	Title identifier	CHAR(3)
au_id	Author identifier	CHAR(3)
au_order	Author name order on book cover	SMALLINT
royalty_share	Author fractional royalty share	DECIMAL(5,2)

Table A.5 Table Structure of *royalties*

Column Name	Description	Data Type
title_id	Unique title identifier	CHAR(3)
advance	Up-front payment to author(s)	DECIMAL(9,2)
royalty_rate	Fraction of revenue paid author(s)	DECIMAL(5,2)

Appendix B

Running SQL Programs

You need a database management system to run SQL programs. You can have your own private copy of a DBMS running on your personal (local) computer, or you can use a shared DBMS over a network. In the latter case, you use your personal computer to connect to a DBMS server running on another machine. The computer where the DBMS is running is called a **host**.

DBMSs and SQL Tools

This appendix describes how to run SQL programs on these DBMSs:

- Microsoft Access
- Microsoft SQL Server
- Oracle
- IBM DB2
- MySQL
- PostgreSQL

Microsoft Access's graphical interface lets you run only one SQL statement at a time. The other systems, all DBMS servers, let you run SQL programs in interactive mode or script mode. In **interactive mode**, you type individual SQL statements at a command prompt and view the results of each statement separately, so input and output are interleaved. In **script mode** (also called **batch mode**), you save your entire SQL program in a text file (called a **script** or a **batch file**), and a command-line tool takes the file, executes the program, and returns the results without your intervention. I describe the minimal syntax of command-line tools; the complete syntax is given in the DBMS documentation.

The Command Line

Most database professionals prefer to submit commands and SQL scripts through a DBMS's command-line environment rather than mousing around the menus and windows of a graphical front-end. (Database administrators don't add 1000 users by pointing and clicking.) If you're new to DBMSs, you might find the command line to be cryptic and intimidating, but experience will show you its power, simplicity, and speed. Graphical tools do have a few advantages, though:

- Full clipboard support for cut, copy, and paste
- Boundless horizontal and vertical scrolling
- Column widths that you can change by dragging with the mouse
- Better history of the commands and results

Command-line addicts can find free full-featured SQL shells that work across DBMSs by searching the web for *sql front end* or *sql client*. Unix lovers stuck with Windows can run popular Unix shells by using Cygwin (*cygwin.com*). Windows PowerShell also provides advanced scripting.

Paths

A **path** (or **pathname**) specifies the unique location of a directory (folder) or file in a filesystem hierarchy. An **absolute path** specifies a location completely, starting at the topmost node of the directory tree, called the **root**. A **relative path** specifies a location relative to the current (or working) directory. In Windows, an absolute path starts with a backslash (\) or with a drive letter followed by a colon and a backslash (C:\, for example). In Unix or Mac OS X Terminal, an absolute path starts with a slash (/).

C:\Program Files\Microsoft SQL Server (Windows) and */usr/local/bin/mysql* (Unix) are absolute paths, for example. *scripts\listing0101.sql* (Windows) and *doc/readme.txt* (Unix) are relative paths. Absolute paths for files and folders on a network also can begin with a double backslash and server name (*someserver*, for example). If a path contains spaces, surround the entire path with double quotes. When you specify the name of an SQL file in script mode, you can include an absolute or relative path.

To run a command-line tool from an arbitrary directory, your **PATH environment variable** must include the directory that actually contains the tool. This environment variable lists the directories (folders) that the OS searches for programs. For some DBMSs, the installer handles the PATH details; for others, you must add the tool's directory to PATH yourself.

To view the contents of the PATH variable, type `path` (Windows) or `echo $PATH` (Unix or Mac OS X Terminal) at a command prompt. To change the PATH, add the absolute path of the directory in which the tool resides to the PATH environment variable. Search Help for *environment variable* (Windows), or modify the path command in your login initialization file, usually named .bash_login, .bashrc, .cshrc, .login, .profile, or .shrc (Unix or Mac OS X).

Microsoft Access

Microsoft Access is a commercial desktop DBMS that supports small and medium-size databases. Learn about Access at *office.microsoft.com/access* and download a free trial copy. This book covers Access 2007 and later but also includes tips for Access 2003 and earlier.

In Access, you must turn on ANSI-92 SQL syntax to run many of the examples in this book.

To turn on ANSI-92 SQL syntax for a database:

1 In Access, open the database if necessary.

2 In Access 2010 or later, choose File tab > Options > Object Designers (in the left pane).

 or

 In Access 2007, choose Microsoft Office Button > Access Options > Object Designers (in the left pane).

 or

 In Access 2003 or earlier, choose Tools > Options > Tables/Queries tab.

3 Below SQL Server Compatible Syntax (ANSI 92), select "This database".

4 Click OK.

 Access closes, compacts, and then reopens the database before the new setting takes effect. You may see a few warnings, depending on your security settings.

ANSI-89 vs. ANSI-92 SQL

Be careful switching between ANSI-89 (the default for Access) and ANSI-92 SQL syntax mode. The modes aren't compatible, so you should pick a mode when you create a database and never change it. The range of data types, reserved words, and wildcard characters differs by mode, so SQL statements created in one mode might not work in the other. The older ANSI-89 standard is limited compared with ANSI-92, so you should choose ANSI-92 syntax for new databases.

DBMS If you're using Access as a front-end to query a **Microsoft SQL Server** database, you must use ANSI-92 syntax. If you're using **Access 97** or earlier, you're stuck with ANSI-89.

If you're a casual Access user, you've probably used the query design grid to create a query. When you create a query in Design View, Access builds the equivalent SQL statement behind the scenes for you. You can view, edit, and run the SQL statement in SQL View.

Tip: You can run only a single SQL statement through an Access Query object. To run multiple statements, use multiple Query objects or a host language such as Visual Basic or C#.

To run an SQL statement in Access 2007 or later:

1. Open a database.
2. In Access 2010 or later, choose Create tab > Queries group > Query Design.

   or

   In Access 2007, choose Create tab > Other group > Query Design.
3. Without adding tables or queries, click Close in the Show Table dialog box.
4. To run the SQL statement, choose Design tab > Results group > SQL View.
5. Type or paste an SQL statement.
6. Choose Design tab > Results group > Run.

   Access displays the result of a SELECT statement but blocks or executes other types of SQL statements, with or without warning messages, depending on your settings.

Tip: To display a list of existing queries in Access 2007 or later, press F11 to show the Navigation pane (on the left), click the menu at the top of the pane and choose Object Type, and then click the menu again and choose Queries. The Navigation pane replaced the Database window of earlier Access versions.

To run an SQL statement in Access 2003 or earlier:

1. Open a database, or press F11 to switch to the Database window for the open database.
2. In the Database window, click Queries (below Objects), and then click New in the toolbar).
3. In the New Query dialog box, click Design View, and then click OK.

4 Without adding tables or queries, click Close in the Show Table dialog box.

5 Choose View > SQL View.

6 Type or paste an SQL statement.

7 To run the SQL statement, click ! on the toolbar or choose Query > Run.

   Access displays the result of a SELECT statement but blocks or executes other types of SQL statements, with or without warning messages, depending on your settings.

Microsoft SQL Server

Microsoft SQL Server is a commercial DBMS that supports very large databases and numbers of transactions. It runs on only Microsoft Windows operating systems and is complex enough to require a full-time database administrator (DBA) to run and maintain it.

Learn about SQL Server products at *microsoft.com/sql* and download a free trial copy of SQL Server or a (permanently) free copy of SQL Server Express. SQL Server Express is a free, easy-to-use, lightweight edition of SQL Server. To run SQL programs in SQL Server or SQL Server Express, you can use the SQL Server Management Studio graphical tool or the **sqlcmd** command-line tool.

This book covers SQL Server 2005 and later but also includes tips for SQL Server 2000 and earlier. To determine which version of Microsoft SQL Server you're running, run the SQL Server command-line command

```
sqlcmd -E -Q "SELECT @@VERSION;"
```

or run the query

```
SELECT SERVERPROPERTY('ProductVersion');
```

or

```
SELECT @@VERSION;
```

In SQL Server 2000 and earlier, the graphical tool is called SQL Query Analyzer, and the command-line tool is osql (which has many of the same command-line options as sqlcmd).

Tip: You can use the SET ANSI_DEFAULTS ON option to make SQL Server conform to standard SQL more closely.

To use SQL Server Management Studio:

1. On the Windows desktop, choose Start > All Programs > Microsoft SQL Server > SQL Server Management Studio.

2. In the Connect to Server dialog box, select the server and authentication mode, and then click Connect.

3. In Object Explorer (the left pane), expand the Databases folder of the server that you're using and then select a database.

   If Object Explorer isn't visible, choose View > Object Explorer (or press F8).

4. To run SQL interactively, click New Query (on the toolbar) or right-click the database (in Object Explorer) and choose New Query, and then type or paste an SQL statement in the empty tab that appears in the right pane.

   or

   To run an SQL script, choose File > Open > File (or press Ctrl+O), navigate to and select the script file, and then click Open. The file's contents appear in a new tab in the right pane.

5. Click Execute (on the toolbar) or choose Query > Execute (or press F5).

   SQL Server displays the result in the bottom pane.

To use the sqlcmd command-line tool interactively:

1. At a command prompt, type:

   ```
   sqlcmd -d dbname
   ```

   dbname is the name of the database to use.

2. Type an SQL statement. The statement can span multiple lines. Terminate it with a semicolon (;) and then press Enter.

3. Type go and then press Enter to display the result.

To use the sqlcmd command-line tool in script mode:

1. At a command prompt, type:

   ```
   sqlcmd -d dbname -i sql_script
   ```

   dbname is the name of the database to use. *sql_script* is a text file containing SQL statement(s) and can include an absolute or relative path.

2. Press Enter to display the result.

To exit the sqlcmd command-line tool:

- Type `exit` or `quit` and then press Enter.

To show sqlcmd command-line options:

- At a command prompt, type `sqlcmd -?` and then press Enter.

sqlcmd tries to use a trusted connection by default. If instead you have to specify a user name and password, add the option `-U` *`login_id`*. *login_id* is your user name. sqlcmd will prompt you for your password.

If SQL Server is running on a remote network computer, add the option `-S` *`server`* to specify the SQL Server instance to connect to. Ask your database administrator for the connection parameters. The `-S` option also works for local connections, when SQL Server is running on your own personal computer rather than on some server elsewhere.

Oracle

Oracle Database is a commercial DBMS that supports very large databases and numbers of transactions. It runs on many operating systems and hardware platforms and is complex enough to require a full-time database administrator (DBA) to run and maintain it.

Learn about Oracle products at *oracle.com* and download Oracle Express Edition (XE)—a free, starter version of Oracle Database. Documentation is at *oracle.com/technetwork/indexes/documentation*.

This book covers Oracle 11g and 12c but also includes tips for Oracle 10g and earlier. To determine which version of Oracle you're running, run the query

```
SELECT banner FROM v$version;
```

The Oracle version also is displayed in the initial "Connected to" message that appears when you log on to SQL*Plus.

To run SQL programs, use the **sqlplus** command-line tool.

To use the sqlplus command-line tool interactively:

1 At a command prompt, type:

   ```
   sqlplus user/password@dbname
   ```

   user is your Oracle user name, *password* is your password, and *dbname* is the name of the database to connect to.

For security, you can omit the password and instead type:

```
sqlplus user@dbname
```

sqlplus will prompt you for your password.

2 Type an SQL statement. The statement can span multiple lines. Terminate it with a semicolon (;) and then press Enter to display the result.

To use the sqlplus command-line tool in script mode:

- At a command prompt, type:

  ```
  sqlplus user/password@dbname @sql_script
  ```

  user is your Oracle user name, *password* is your password, *dbname* is the name of the database to connect to, and *sql_script* is a text file containing SQL statement(s) and can include an absolute or relative path. For security, you can omit the password, and instead type:

  ```
  sqlplus user@dbname @sql_script
  ```

  sqlplus will prompt you for your password.

To exit the sqlplus command-line tool:

- Type `exit` or `quit` and then press Enter.

To show sqlplus command-line options:

- At a command prompt, type `sqlplus -H` and then press Enter.

  This command displays a few pages that speed by. To view one page at a time, type

  ```
  sqlplus -H | more
  ```

  and then press Enter. Tap the spacebar to advance pages.

If you're running Oracle locally, you can use the user name system and the password you specified when you created the database:

```
sqlplus system@dbname
```

If you're connecting to a remote Oracle database, ask your database administrator for the connection parameters.

An alternative way to open sqlplus in Windows: choose Start > All Programs > Oracle > Application Development > SQL Plus.

IBM DB2

IBM DB2 is a commercial DBMS that supports very large databases and numbers of transactions. It runs on many operating systems and hardware platforms and is complex enough to require a full-time database administrator (DBA) to run and maintain it.

Learn about DB2 products at *ibm.com/db2* and download a free trial copy of DB2 or a (permanently) free copy of IBM DB2 Express-C.

This book covers DB2 9 and 10 but also includes tips for DB2 8 and earlier. To determine which version of DB2 you're running, run the DB2 command-line command

```
db2level
```

or run the query

```
SELECT service_level
  FROM SYSIBMADM.ENV_INST_INFO;
```

To run SQL programs, use the IBM Data Studio graphical tool (DB2 10), the Command Editor graphical tool (DB2 9), the Command Center graphical tool (DB2 8), or the **db2** command-line processor (CLP).

To use Data Studio (DB2 10):

1 Open Data Studio.

   This procedure varies by platform. In Windows, for example, choose Start > All Programs > IBM Data Studio > Data Studio Client.

2 On the Administration Explorer tab (on the left), expand the All Databases folder of the object tree until you find your instance of DB2, and then choose a database (below the DB2 instance).

   If the desired database doesn't appear, right-click the All Databases folder, choose New Connection to a Database from the shortcut menu, and then connect to the target database.

3 To run SQL interactively, click New SQL Script on the Administration Explorer toolbar. On the Script tab that opens, type or paste an SQL statement in the box.

   or

   To run an SQL script, choose File > Open File, navigate to and select the script file, and then click Open. On the File tab that opens, click No Connection (if it appears) to connect to the target database.

4 Choose Run > Run SQL or click .

Data Studio displays the result in the SQL Results tab (at the bottom). Click the Result tab to see the query result or click the Status tab to see query-processing information.

To use Command Editor (DB2 9):

1 Open Command Editor.

This procedure varies by platform. In Windows, for example, choose Start > All Programs > IBM DB2 > [*db2_copy_name*] > Command Line Tools > Command Editor. In Unix and Linux, use the command `db2ce`.

Alternatively, if Control Center is open, choose Tools > Command Editor or click .

2 On the Commands tab, choose a database in the Target list.

If the desired database doesn't appear in the Target list, click Add (to the right of the list), choose a database, and then click OK.

3 To run SQL interactively, type or paste an SQL statement in the top box of the Commands tab.

or

To run an SQL script, choose Selected > Open (or press Ctrl+O), navigate to and select the script file, and then click OK.

4 Click or press Ctrl+Enter.

or

Choose Selected > Execute.

Command Editor displays the result in the Query Results tab. The bottom box of the Commands tab shows query-processing information.

To use Command Center (DB2 8):

1 Open Command Center.

This procedure varies by platform. In Windows, for example, choose Start > All Programs > IBM DB2 > Command Line Tools > Command Center. In Unix and Linux, use the command `db2cctr`.

Alternatively, if Control Center is open, choose Tools > Command Center or click .

2 Choose the command-type SQL Statements and DB2 CLP Commands.

3 Click the Interactive tab.

4 In the Database Connection box, click ..., expand the object tree until you find the Databases folder, select a database, and then click OK.

5 To run SQL interactively, in the Command box, type or paste an SQL statement.

or

To run an SQL script, click the Scripts tab, choose Script > Import, navigate to and select the script file, and then click OK.

6 Click or press Ctrl+Enter.

or

Choose Interactive > Execute or Script > Execute.

Interactive-SQL results appear in the Results tab. SQL-script results appear in the box below the Script box.

For technical reasons involving parent and child processes, (only) Microsoft Windows users must start the db2 command-line processor with a special preliminary step.

To start the db2 command-line processor in Windows:

- At a command prompt, type `db2cmd` and then press Enter.

  or

  For DB2 10, choose Start > All Programs > IBM DB2 DB2COPY1 (Default) > DB2 Command Line Processor.

  or

  For DB2 9, choose Start > All Programs > IBM DB2 > [*db2_copy_name*] > Command Line Tools > Command Window.

  or

  For DB2 8, choose Start > All Programs > IBM DB2 > Command Line Tools > Command Window.

  A new DB2 CLP command-prompt window appears.

You must use the DB2 CLP window for all db2 commands (described next). If you try to run db2 at a regular Windows command prompt, DB2 responds with the error "Command line environment not initialized."

If you launch a new DB2 CLP window via the db2cmd command, you can close the original command-prompt window.

In the DB2 CLP window, change (cd) your working directory if necessary before you run db2 commands.

To use the db2 command-line processor interactively:

1. At a command prompt, type:

   ```
   db2 -t
   ```

   and then press Enter. The -t option tells db2 that a semicolon (;) terminates statements.

   The db2 => prompt appears.

2. At the db2 prompt, type:

   ```
   connect to dbname;
   ```

   and then press Enter. *dbname* is the name of the database to use.

3. Type an SQL statement. The statement can span multiple lines. Terminate it with a semicolon and then press Enter to display the results.

Alternatively, you can avoid the db2 => prompt by typing commands and SQL statements right on the command line. For example:

```
db2 connect to books
```

```
db2 SELECT * FROM authors
```

If you omit the -t option, as here, don't terminate commands and SQL statements with a semicolon.

To use the db2 command-line processor in script mode:

1. At a command prompt, type:

   ```
   db2 connect to dbname
   ```

   dbname is the name of the database to use.

2. At a command prompt, type:

   ```
   db2 -t -f sql_script
   ```

   sql_script is a text file containing SQL statement(s) and can include an absolute or relative path. The -t option tells db2 that a semicolon (;) terminates statements. Add the -v option if you want to echo the contents of *sql_script* in the output.

3. Press Enter to display the results.

Tip: An alternative script tool is db2batch.

To exit the db2 command-line tool:

- At the db2 prompt, type `quit;` and then press Enter. (Omit the semicolon if you didn't use the -t option when you started db2.)

To show db2 command-line options:

- At a command prompt, type `db2 ?` and then press Enter.

  This command displays a few pages that speed by quickly. To view one page at a time, instead type

  ```
  db2 ? | more
  ```

  and then press Enter. Tap the spacebar to advance pages.

  To get help while you're at a db2 => prompt, type `?;` and then press Enter. (Omit the semicolon if you didn't use the -t option when you started db2.)

Tip: DB2 for Linux, Unix, and Windows ("LUW" in IBM-speak) differs somewhat from DB2 on other platforms. This section covers LUW DB2. If you're running non-LUW DB2 (on z/OS or OS/390, for example), your commands might differ.

MySQL

MySQL (pronounced *my-es-kyoo-el*) is an open-source DBMS that supports large databases and numbers of transactions. MySQL is known for its speed and ease of use. It's free for personal use and runs on many operating systems and hardware platforms. You can download it at *mysql.com*.

This book covers MySQL 5 but also includes tips for MySQL 4 and earlier. To determine which version of MySQL you're running, run the MySQL command-line command

```
mysql -V
```

or run the query

```
SELECT VERSION();
```

To run SQL programs, use the **mysql** command-line tool.

To use the mysql command-line tool interactively:

1 At a command prompt, type:

```
mysql -h host -u user -p dbname
```

host is the host name, *user* is your MySQL user name, and *dbname* is the name of the database to use. MySQL will prompt you for your password (for a passwordless user, either omit the -p option or press Enter at the password prompt).

2 Type an SQL statement. The statement can span multiple lines. Terminate it with a semicolon (;) and then press Enter to display the results.

To use the mysql command-line tool in script mode:

1 At a command prompt, type (on one line):

```
mysql -h host -u user -p -t
  dbname < sql_script
```

host is the host name, *user* is your MySQL user name, and *dbname* is the name of the database to use. MySQL will prompt you for your password (for a passwordless user, either omit the -p option or press Enter at the password prompt). The -t option formats the results as a table; omit this option if you want tab-delimited output. The < redirection operator reads from the file *sql_script*, which is a text file containing SQL statement(s) and can include an absolute or relative path.

2 Press Enter to display the results.

To exit the mysql command-line tool:

- Type `quit` or `\q` and then press Enter.

To show mysql command-line options:

- At a command prompt, type `mysql -?` and then press Enter.

  This command displays a few pages that speed by. To view one page at a time, type

  ```
  mysql -? | more
  ```

  and then press Enter. Tap the spacebar to advance pages.

If MySQL is running on a remote network computer, ask your database administrator for the connection parameters. If you're running MySQL locally (that is, on your own computer), then set *host* to `localhost`, set *user* to `root`, and use the password you assigned to root when you set up MySQL.

PostgreSQL

PostgreSQL (pronounced *post-gres-kyoo-el*) is an open-source DBMS that supports large databases and numbers of transactions. PostgreSQL is known for its rich feature set and its high conformance with standard SQL. It's free and runs on many operating systems and hardware platforms. You can download it at *postgresql.org*.

This book covers PostgreSQL 9 but also includes tips for PostgreSQL 8 and earlier. To determine which version of PostgreSQL you're running, run the PostgreSQL command-line command

```
psql -V
```

or run the query

```
SELECT VERSION();
```

To run SQL programs, use the **psql** command-line tool.

To use the psql command-line tool interactively:

1 At a command prompt, type:

```
psql -h host -U user -W dbname
```

host is the host name, *user* is your PostgreSQL user name, and *dbname* is the name of the database to use. PostgreSQL will prompt you for your password (for a passwordless user, either omit the -W option or press Enter at the password prompt).

2 Type an SQL statement. The statement can span multiple lines. Terminate it with a semicolon (;) and then press Enter to display the results.

To use the psql command-line tool in script mode:

1 At a command prompt, type (on one line):

```
psql -h host -U user -W
  -f sql_script dbname
```

host is the host name, *user* is your PostgreSQL user name, and *dbname* is the name of the database to use. PostgreSQL will prompt you for your password (for a passwordless user, either omit the -W option or press Enter at the password prompt). The -f option specifies the name of the SQL file *sql_script*, which is a text file containing SQL statement(s) and can include an absolute or relative path.

2 Press Enter to display the results.

To exit the psql command-line tool:

- Type `\q` and then press Enter.

To show psql command-line options:

- At a command prompt, type `psql -?` and then press Enter.

  This command displays a few pages that speed by. To view one page at a time, type

  ```
  psql -? | more
  ```

  and then press Enter. Tap the spacebar to advance pages.

If PostgreSQL is running on a remote network computer, ask your database administrator for the connection parameters. If you're running PostgreSQL locally (that is, on your own computer), then set *host* to `localhost`, set *user* to `postgres`, and use the password you assigned to postgres when you set up PostgreSQL.

You can set the environment variables PGDATABASE and PGUSER to specify the default database and the user name used to connect to the database. See *Environment Variables* in the PostgreSQL documentation.

Tip: As an alternative to the command prompt, you can use the pgAdmin graphical tool. If the PostgreSQL installer didn't install pgAdmin automatically, you can download it for free at *pgadmin.org*.

Appendix C

Data Types

Data types are essentially rules that define which data values can be stored in a column and how those values are actually stored.

Data Types

Recall from "Columns" on page 10 that a domain is the set of valid values allowed in a column. To define a domain, you use a column's data type (and constraints). A **data type**, or **column type**, has these characteristics:

- Each column in a table has a single data type.
- A data type falls into one of categories listed in Table C.1 (each covered in the following sections).
- The data type determines a column's allowable values and the operations it supports. An integer data type, for example, can represent any whole number between certain DBMS-defined limits and supports the usual arithmetic operations: addition, subtraction, multiplication, and division (among others). But an integer can't represent a nonnumeric value such as 'john' and doesn't support character operations such as capitalization and concatenation.
- The data type affects the column's sort order. The integers 1, 2, and 10 are sorted numerically, yielding 1, 2, 10. The character strings '1', '2', and '10' are sorted lexicographically, yielding '1', '10', '2'. **Lexicographical ordering** sorts strings by examining the values of their characters individually. Here, '10' comes before '2' because '1' (the first character of '10') is less than '2' lexicographically. For information about sorting, see Chapter 5.
- You store **literal values** (constants) in character, numeric, Boolean, and datetime columns. Table C.2 shows some examples; the following sections have more examples. Be sure not to confuse the string literal *'2009'* with the numeric literal *2009*. The SQL standard defines a literal as any constant that isn't null.

Table C.1 Categories of Data Types

Category	Stores These Data
Character string	Strings of characters
Binary large object	Binary data
Exact numeric	Integers and decimal numbers
Approximate numeric	Floating-point numbers
Boolean	Truth values: true, false, or unknown
Datetime	Date and time values

Tips for data types

- The CREATE TABLE and ALTER TABLE statements define and change a column's data type; see Chapter 21.
- Database designers choose data types carefully. The consequences of a poor data-type choice include the inability to insert values into a column and data loss if the existing data type must be changed.
- The SQL:2003 standard dropped SQL-92's bit-string data types (BIT and BIT VARYING) in favor of binary large objects. Bit strings held smaller binary-data items than BLOBs do.
- **DBMS** The SQL standard leaves many data-type implementation details up to the DBMS vendor. Consequently, SQL data types don't map directly to specific DBMS data types, even if the data types have identical names. I give equivalent or similar DBMS data types in the Tips of each of the following data-type sections. Some DBMS data types have synonyms that match the SQL standard's data-type names.

Table C.2 Examples of Literals

Literal	Examples
Character string	`'42', 'ennui', 'don''t', N'John'`
Numeric	`42, 12.34, 2., .001, -123, +6.33333, 2.5E2, 5E-3`
Boolean	`TRUE, FALSE, UNKNOWN`
Datetime	`DATE '2005-06-22', TIME '09:45:00', TIMESTAMP '2006-10-19 10:23:54'`

Character String Types

Use character string data types to represent text. A **character string**, or simply **string**, has these characteristics:

- It's an ordered sequence of zero or more characters.
- Its length can be fixed or varying.
- It's case sensitive ('A' comes before 'a' when sorted).
- In SQL statements, a string is surrounded by single quotes.
- It's one of the types listed in Table C.3.

Table C.3 Character String Types

Type	Description
CHARACTER	Represents a fixed number of characters. A string stored in a column defined as CHARACTER(*length*) can have up to *length* characters, where *length* is an integer greater than or equal to 1; the maximum *length* depends on the DBMS. When you store a string with fewer than *length* characters in a CHARACTER(*length*) column, the DBMS pads the end of the string with spaces to create a string that has exactly *length* characters. A CHARACTER(6) string 'John' is stored as 'John ', for example. CHARACTER and CHAR are synonyms.
CHARACTER VARYING	Represents a variable number of characters. A string stored in a column defined as CHARACTER VARYING(*length*) can have up to *length* characters, where *length* is an integer greater than or equal to 1; the maximum *length* depends on the DBMS. Unlike CHARACTER, when you store a string with fewer than *length* characters in a CHARACTER VARYING(*length*) column, the DBMS stores the string as is and doesn't pad it with spaces. A CHARACTER VARYING(6) string 'John' is stored as 'John', for example. CHARACTER VARYING, CHAR VARYING, and VARCHAR are synonyms.

Type	Description
NATIONAL CHARACTER	This data type is the same as CHARACTER except that it holds standardized multibyte characters or Unicode characters. In SQL statements, NATIONAL CHARACTER strings are written like CHARACTER strings but have an N in front of the first quote: N'ßæþ', for example. NATIONAL CHARACTER, NATIONAL CHAR, and NCHAR are synonyms.
NATIONAL CHARACTER VARYING	This data type is the same as CHARACTER VARYING except that it holds standardized multibyte characters or Unicode characters (see NATIONAL CHARACTER). NATIONAL CHARACTER VARYING, NATIONAL CHAR VARYING, and NCHAR VARYING are synonyms.
CLOB	The character large object (CLOB) type is intended for use in library databases that hold vast amounts of text. A single CLOB value might hold an entire webpage, book, or genetic sequence, for example. CLOBs can't be used as keys or in indexes and support fewer functions and operations than do CHAR and VARCHAR. In host languages, CLOBs are referenced with a unique locator (pointer) value, avoiding the overhead of transferring entire CLOBs across a client–server network. CLOB and CHARACTER LARGE OBJECT are synonyms.
NCLOB	The national character large object (NCLOB) type is the same as CLOB except that it holds standardized multibyte characters or Unicode characters (see NATIONAL CHARACTER). NCLOB, NCHAR LARGE OBJECT, and NATIONAL CHARACTER LARGE OBJECT are synonyms.

Tips for character strings

- Two consecutive single quotes represent one single-quote character in a string. Type 'don''t' to represent don't, for example. A double-quote character (") is a separate character and doesn't need this special treatment.
- The length of a string is an integer between 0 and *length*, inclusive. A string with no characters—'' (two single quotes with no intervening space)—is called an **empty string** or a **zero-length string**. An empty string is considered to be a VARCHAR of length zero.
- DBMSs often can sort and manipulate fixed-length strings faster than variable-length ones.
- Keep character columns as short as possible rather than giving them "room to grow" in the future. Shorter columns sort and group faster than longer ones.
- The SQL:1999 standard introduced CLOB and NCLOB to the SQL language (but most DBMSs already had similar data types by then).
- **DBMS** Table C.4 lists character-string and similar types for the DBMSs. See the DBMS documentation for size limits and usage restrictions.

  Oracle treats empty strings as nulls; see "Nulls" on page 22.

  In **MySQL** ANSI_QUOTES mode, string literals can be quoted only with single quotes; a string quoted with double quotes is interpreted as an identifier.

Table C.4 DBMS Character String Types

DBMS	Types
Access	text, memo (in Access 2013 and later: short text, long text)
SQL Server	char, nchar, ntext, nvarchar, text, varchar
Oracle	char, varchar2, nchar, nvarchar2, clob, nclob, long
DB2	char, varchar, long varchar, clob, dbclob, graphic, vargraphic, long vargraphic, binary, varbinary
MySQL	char, varchar, national char, national varchar, tinytext, text, mediumtext, longtext
PostgreSQL	char, varchar, text

Unicode

Computers store characters (letters, digits, punctuation, control characters, and other symbols) internally by assigning them unique numeric values. An **encoding** determines the mapping of characters to numeric values; different languages and computer operating systems use many different native encodings. Standard U.S.-English strings use **ASCII** encoding, which assigns values to 128 (2^7) different characters—not much, and not even enough to hold all the Latin characters used in modern European languages, much less all the Chinese ideographs.

Unicode is a single character set that represents the characters of almost all the world's written languages. Unicode can encode up to about 4.3 billion (2^{32}) characters (using UTF-32 encoding). The Unicode Consortium develops and maintains the Unicode standard. The actual Unicode mappings are available in the latest online or printed edition of *The Unicode Standard*, available at *unicode.org*.

Binary Large Object Type

Use the **binary large object** (**BLOB**) data type to store binary data. A BLOB has these characteristics:

- The type name is BLOB or BINARY LARGE OBJECT.
- Unlike a CLOB, which stores a long character string, a BLOB stores a long sequence of bytes. The two data types are incompatible.
- BLOBs are used mainly to store large amounts of multimedia data (graphics, photos, audio, or video, for example), scientific data (medical images or climate maps), or technical data (engineering drawings).
- BLOBs can't be used as keys or in indexes and support far fewer functions and operations than do other types. BLOBs can be compared for only equality (=) or inequality (<>) because it makes no sense for a BLOB to be "less than" another BLOB. You also can't use BLOBs with DISTINCT, in GROUP BY or ORDER BY clauses, or in column functions.
- In host languages, BLOBs are referenced with a unique **locator** (pointer) value, avoiding the overhead of transferring entire BLOBs across a client/server network.

Tips for binary large objects

- DBMSs don't attempt to interpret BLOBs; their meaning is up to the application.
- A binary string literal is given in **hexadecimal**, or **hex** (base 16), format. The hexadecimal system uses the digits 0 through 9 and the letters *A* through *F* (uppercase or lowercase). One hex character is equivalent to 4 bits. In SQL statements, hex strings have an X in front of the first quote, with no intervening space. The hex string X'4B' corresponds to the bits 01001011 or the **bit string** B'01001011', for example.
- The SQL:1999 standard introduced BLOB to the SQL language (but most DBMSs already had similar data types by then).
- **DBMS** Table C.5 lists BLOB and similar types for the DBMSs. See the DBMS documentation for size limits and usage restrictions.

Table C.5 DBMS BLOB Types

DBMS	Types
Access	ole object, attachment
SQL Server	binary, image, varbinary
Oracle	raw, long raw, blob, bfile
DB2	blob
MySQL	binary, varbinary, tinyblob, blob, mediumblob, longblob
PostgreSQL	bit, bit varying, bytea, oid

Exact Numeric Types

Use exact numeric data types to represent exact numerical values. An **exact numerical value** has these characteristics:

- It can be a negative, zero, or positive number.
- It's an integer or a decimal number. An **integer** is a whole number expressed without a decimal point: −42, 0, 62262. A **decimal number** has digits to the right of the decimal point: −22.06, 0.0, 0.0003, 12.34.
- It has a fixed precision and scale. The **precision** is the number of significant digits used to express the number; it's the total number of digits both to the right and to the left of the decimal point. The **scale** is the number of digits to the right of the decimal point. Obviously, the scale can't exceed the precision. To represent a whole number, set the scale equal to zero. Table C.6 shows how the number 123.89 is stored for different precision and scale values.
- It's one of the types listed in Table C.7.

Table C.6 Precision and Scale Examples for 123.89

Specified As	Stored As
`NUMERIC(5)`	`124`
`NUMERIC(5,0)`	`124`
`NUMERIC(5,1)`	`123.9`
`NUMERIC(5,2)`	`123.89`
`NUMERIC(4,0)`	`124`
`NUMERIC(4,1)`	`123.9`
`NUMERIC(4,2)`	Exceeds precision
`NUMERIC(2,0)`	Exceeds precision

Table C.7 Exact Numeric Types

Type	Description
NUMERIC	Represents a decimal number, stored in a column defined as NUMERIC(*precision* [,*scale*]). *precision* is greater than or equal to 1; the maximum *precision* depends on the DBMS. *scale* is a value from 0 to *precision*. If *scale* is omitted, it defaults to zero (which makes the number effectively an INTEGER).
DECIMAL	This data type is similar to NUMERIC, and some DBMSs define them equivalently. The difference is that the DBMS can choose a *precision* greater than that specified by DECIMAL(*precision* [,*scale*]), so *precision* specifies the minimum precision, not an exact precision as in NUMERIC. DECIMAL and DEC are synonyms.
INTEGER	Represents an integer. The minimum and maximum values that can be stored in an INTEGER column depend on the DBMS. INTEGER takes no arguments. INTEGER and INT are synonyms.
SMALLINT	This data type is the same as INTEGER except that it might hold a smaller range of values, depending on the DBMS. SMALLINT takes no arguments.
BIGINT	This data type is the same as INTEGER except that it might hold a larger range of values, depending on the DBMS. BIGINT takes no arguments.

Tips for exact numeric types

- Don't enclose a numeric literal in quotes.
- Store numbers as strings if the numbers are not involved in arithmetic calculations. Store telephone numbers, credit-card numbers, postal codes, and U.S. Social Security numbers as strings, for example. This technique can save space and prevent data loss: if you store the postal code '02116' as a number instead of as a string, you'll lose the leading zero.
- Calculations involving only integers are much faster than those involving decimal and floating-point numbers.
- **DBMS** Table C.8 lists exact-numeric and similar types for the DBMSs. See the DBMS documentation for size limits and usage restrictions. DBMSs often accept type names that they don't implement, converting them to suitable, supported types; **Oracle** converts INT to NUMBER(32), for example.

  DBMSs usually implement SMALLINT as 16-bit values (−32,768 through 32,767), INTEGER as 32-bit values (−2,147,483,648 through 2,147,483,647), and BIGINT as 64-bit values (quintillions). The SQL:2003 standard introduced BIGINT to the SQL language (but most DBMSs already had a similar data type by then).

Table C.8 DBMS Exact Numeric Types

DBMS	Types
Access	byte, decimal, integer, long integer
SQL Server	int, tinyint, smallint, bigint, bit, numeric, decimal
Oracle	number, float
DB2	smallint, integer, bigint, numeric, decimal
MySQL	tinyint, smallint, mediumint, int, bigint, numeric, decimal
PostgreSQL	smallint, integer, bigint, numeric, decimal

Approximate Numeric Types

Use approximate numeric data types to represent approximate numerical values. An **approximate numerical value** has these characteristics:

- It can be a negative, zero, or positive number.
- It's considered to be an approximation of a floating-point (real) number.
- It typically is used to represent the very small or very large quantities common in technical, scientific, statistical, and financial calculations.
- It's expressed in scientific notation. A number in **scientific notation** is written as a decimal number multiplied by an (integer) power of 10. An uppercase *E* is the exponentiation symbol: 2.5E2 = $2.5 \times 10^2 = 250$, for example. The **mantissa** is the portion that expresses the significant digits (2.5 here), and the **exponent** is the power of 10 (2 here). The mantissa and exponent each can have a sign: –2.5E–2 = $-2.5 \times 10^{-2} = -0.025$.
- It has a fixed precision but no explicit scale. (The sign and magnitude of the exponent determine the scale intrinsically.) The precision is the number of (binary) bits used to store the mantissa. To convert from binary to decimal precision, multiply the precision by 0.30103. To convert from decimal to binary precision, multiply the decimal precision by 3.32193. For example, 24 bits yields 7 digits of precision, and 53 bits yields 15 digits of precision.
- It's one of the types listed in Table C.9.

Table C.9 Approximate Numeric Types

Type	Description
FLOAT	Represents a floating-point number, stored in a column defined as FLOAT(*precision*). *precision* is greater than or equal to 1 and expressed as the number of bits (not the number of digits); the maximum *precision* depends on the DBMS.
REAL	This data type is the same as FLOAT except that the DBMS defines the precision. REAL numbers usually are called single-precision numbers. REAL takes no arguments.
DOUBLE PRECISION	This data type is the same as FLOAT except that the DBMS defines the precision, which must be greater than that of REAL. DOUBLE PRECISION takes no arguments.

Tips for approximate numeric types

- Don't enclose a numeric literal in quotes.
- DBMS Table C.10 lists approximate numeric and similar types for the DBMSs. See the DBMS documentation for size limits and usage restrictions. DBMSs often accept type names that they don't implement, converting them to suitable, supported types; **PostgreSQL** converts float to double precision, for example.

Table C.10 DBMS Approximate Numeric Types

DBMS	Types
Access	single, double
SQL Server	float, real
Oracle	binary_float, binary_double
DB2	real, double, decfloat
MySQL	float, double
PostgreSQL	real, double precision

Boolean Type

Use the Boolean data type to store truth values. A **Boolean value** has these characteristics:

- The type name is BOOLEAN.
- The truth values are True, False, and Unknown, represented by the Boolean literals TRUE, FALSE, and UNKNOWN. Truth values are described in Chapter 7.
- A null is equivalent to the Unknown truth value and, in practice, usually is used instead of Unknown (most DBMS Boolean types don't accept the literal UNKNOWN). See "Nulls" on page 22.

Tips for Boolean values

- Don't enclose a Boolean literal in quotes.
- The SQL:1999 standard introduced BOOLEAN to the SQL language.
- **DBMS** Table C.11 lists Boolean and similar types for the DBMSs. See the DBMS documentation for size limits and usage restrictions. Where no Boolean type is available, I give the data type for storing single bits or small integers. SQL programmers often use these numeric values to represent truth values, where zero means false, 1 (or any nonzero number) means true, and null means unknown.

Table C.11 DBMS Boolean Types

DBMS	Types
Access	yes/no
SQL Server	bit
Oracle	number(1)
DB2	decimal(1)
MySQL	boolean, bit, tinyint(1)
PostgreSQL	boolean

Datetime Types

Use datetime data types to represent the date and time of day. **Datetime values** have these characteristics:

- They're specified with respect to UTC, or Universal Coordinated Time (formerly called Greenwich Mean Time or GMT). The SQL standard requires that every SQL session have a default offset from UTC that is used for the duration of the session; −8 hours is the time-zone offset of San Francisco, California, for example.
- The rules of the Gregorian calendar determine how date values are formed. DBMSs reject values that they can't recognize as dates.
- Time values are based on a 24-hour clock, also called military time (use 13:00, not 1:00 p.m.).
- Hyphens (-) separate the parts of a date, and colons (:) separate the parts of a time. A space separates a date and time when both are combined.
- It's one of the types listed in Table C.12.

Table C.12 Datetime Types

Type	Description
TIME	Represents a time of day. A time stored in a column defined as TIME has three fields—HOUR, MINUTE, and SECOND—and is formatted *hh:mm:ss* (length 8) (22:06:57, for example). You can specify fractional seconds with TIME(*precision*). *precision* is the number of fractional digits and is greater than or equal to zero. The maximum *precision*, which is at least 6, depends on the DBMS. HOUR and MINUTE are integers, and SECOND is a decimal number. The format is *hh:mm:ss.ssss...* (length 9 plus the number fractional digits) (22:06:57.1333, for example). Table C.13 lists the valid values for the fields.

Type	Description
DATE	Represents a date. A date stored in a column defined as DATE has three integer fields—YEAR, MONTH, and DAY—and is formatted *yyyy-mm-dd* (length 10) (2006-03-17, for example). Table C.13 lists the valid values for the fields. DATE takes no arguments.
TIMESTAMP	Represents a combination of DATE and TIME values separated by a space. The TIMESTAMP format is *yyyy-mm-dd hh:mm:ss* (length 19) (2006-03-17 22:06:57, for example). You can specify fractional seconds with TIMESTAMP(*precision*). The format is *yyyy-mm-dd hh:mm:ss.ssss...* (length 20 plus the number fractional digits).
TIME WITH TIMEZONE	This data type is the same as TIME except that it adds a field, TIME_ZONE_OFFSET, to indicate the offset in hours from UTC. TIME_ZONE_OFFSET is formatted as shown in Table C.13. Append AT TIME ZONE *time_zone_offset* to the TIME to assign a value to the time zone (22:06:57 AT TIME ZONE -08:00, for example). Alternatively, you can append AT LOCAL to indicate that the time zone is the default for the session (22:06:57 AT LOCAL, for example). If the AT clause is omitted, all times default to AT LOCAL.
TIMESTAMP WITH TIMEZONE	This data type is the same as TIMESTAMP except that it adds a field, TIME_ZONE_OFFSET, to indicate the offset in hours from UTC. The syntax rules are the same as those of TIME WITH TIME ZONE except that you must include a date (2006-03-17 22:06:57 AT TIME ZONE -08:00, for example).

Tips for datetime values

- To get your system time, see Table 11.2 on page 76.
- You can compare two datetime values if they have the same fields. See "Performing Datetime and Interval Arithmetic" on page 74.
- The SECOND field in Table C.13 can accept values up to 61.999... (instead of 59) to allow for the (rare) insertion of **leap seconds** into a particular minute to keep Earth's clocks synchronized with sidereal time.
- A datetime literal is a datetime type name, followed by a space, followed by a datetime value surrounded by single quotes—DATE '*yyyy-mm-dd*', TIME '*hh:mm:ss*', and TIMESTAMP '*yyyy-mm-dd hh:mm:ss*', for example.
- Standard SQL can't handle B.C.E./B.C. (Before the Common Era/Before Christ) dates, but your DBMS might be able to do so.
- Timestamps often are used to mark events associated with the row in which they appear. In **MySQL**, for example, a *timestamp* column is useful for recording the date and time of an UPDATE operation.
- The data type TIME WITH TIME ZONE doesn't make sense, because real-world time zones have no meaning unless they're associated with a date (because the time-zone offset varies throughout the year). Favor TIMESTAMP WITH TIME ZONE.
- **DBMS** Table C.14 lists datetime and similar types for the DBMSs. See the DBMS documentation for size limits and usage restrictions.

  DBMSs let you enter date values in month-day-year, day-month-year, and other formats and time values based on a 12-hour (a.m./p.m.) clock. The format in which dates and times are displayed can differ from the format in which they're entered.

  In **Microsoft Access**, surround datetime literals with # characters instead of quotes and omit the data type name prefix. The standard SQL date DATE '2006-03-17' is equivalent to the Access date #2006-03-17#, for example.

  In **Microsoft SQL Server**, omit the data type name prefix from datetime literals. The standard SQL date DATE '2006-03-17' is equivalent to the SQL Server date '2006-03-17', for example.

  In **DB2**, omit the data type name prefix from datetime literals. The standard SQL date DATE '2006-03-17' is equivalent to the DB2 date '2006-03-17', for example.

Table C.13 Valid Values for Datetime Fields

Field	Valid Values
YEAR	0001 to 9999
MONTH	01 to 12
DAY	01 to 31
HOUR	00 to 23
MINUTE	00 to 59
SECOND	00 to 61.999
TIME_ZONE_OFFSET	-12:59 to +13:00

Table C.14 DBMS Datetime Types

DBMS	Types
Access	date/time
SQL Server	date, datetime, datetime2, datetimeoffset, smalldatetime, time
Oracle	date, timestamp
DB2	date, time, timestamp
MySQL	date, time, datetime, timestamp, year
PostgreSQL	date, time, timestamp

Unique Identifiers

Unique identifiers are used to generate primary-key values to identify rows (see "Primary Keys" on page 11). An identifier can be unique universally (large random numbers unique in any context) or only within a specific table (simple serial numbers 1, 2, 3,...). Table C.15 lists unique-identifier types and attributes for the DBMSs. See the DBMS documentation for size limits and usage restrictions. The SQL standard calls columns with auto-incrementing values **identity columns**.

Table C.15 Unique Identifiers (Type or Attribute)

DBMS	Types
Standard SQL	IDENTITY
Access	autonumber, replication id
SQL Server	uniqueidentifier, identity
Oracle	rowid, urowid, sequences
DB2	rowid, identity columns and sequences
MySQL	auto_increment attribute
PostgreSQL	smallserial, serial, bigserial, uuid

Other Data Types

The SQL standard defines other data types than the ones covered in the preceding sections, but some of them rarely are implemented or used in practice (ARRAY, MULTISET, REF, and ROW, for example). More useful are the extended (nonstandard) data types that are available in various DBMSs. Depending on your DBMS, you can find data types for time intervals; network and internet addresses; links to files stored outside the database; monetary (currency) amounts; geographic (spatial) coordinates; arrays and other collections; XML; full text searching; enumerated (enum) values from a specified list; and position in a hierarchy.

Index

Symbols

A

B

C

D

E

F

T

CPSIA information can be obtained at www.ICGtesting.com
Printed in the USA
LVOW04s1504280915

456036LV00015B/832/P

9 781937 84233